HERETICS, HERMITS, BISHOPS AND KINGS

A short history of the Celtic Church.

Pat Robson

Intercelt
intercelt@aol.com

ISBN 978-0-9557727-2-6

Printed by:
Booths Print
The Praze
Penryn
01326 373628

ABOUT THE AUTHOR

Pat Robson was Head of Religious Education at the Humphry Davy Boy's Grammar School in Penzance before training for the priesthood. After working as a Parish Priest in the Diocese of Truro, she is now retired and living in Cornwall.

Her other books include The Celtic Heart (Harper Collins and SPCK), A Celtic Liturgy (Harper Collins and SPCK), Celtic Praise (Tim Tiley Publications) and Son of God (Intercelt).

With thanks to Mary Abbott for her encouragement
and for her many arduous hours of proof reading!

CHAPTER ONE

Setting the scene...

When a young carpenter from Nazareth died in the year AD 33, he left nothing behind him except the seed of a momentous, and seemingly outrageous, hope in the hearts of family and friends who had loved him dearly. The young man's name was Jesus, or Yeshua in the local Aramaic tongue, and it meant 'Saviour', and the hope he had passed on to his followers was a precious gift destined to save mankind. It had been given to a group of Galilean peasants, carpenters, builders and fishermen, all uneducated, simple folk who lived simple lives with their families in a backwater of civilisation.

Surely, after his death, these friends would return to their lives and the precious hope they had been entrusted with, would die.

But, strangely, the opposite happened. His friends did not return to Galilee to live out their lives in obscurity. Instead, each set out with great determination to tell the story and spread the good news of this great hope. The good news that the great Creator God loved His creation so much that he chose to come and live among his beloved people and share their lives. That he chose, too, to die the terrible death of a criminal, in full view of hundreds of people. But then, three days later he miraculously came back to life again to show them that death was not the all powerful enemy they greatly feared, instead it was the gateway to a new and more glorious life where the souls of all would be welcomed into the Kingdom of God.

Because of the work of his disciples the seeds of this incredible hope were sown and began to grow. Those who responded became known as Christians and they were often derided for being fools and criticised for the wildness of their hopes. They were made scapegoats when culprits were needed and they suffered from almost continual persecution. But despite it all, the hope in the hearts of these new Christians refused to die.

Then in AD 312 the unexpected happened. Constantine the Roman Emperor, became a Christian and everything changed. He made Christianity the state religion and suddenly, all over the Empire, from the Scottish borders in the far north west to the southern borders of Egypt, everyone wanted to become a Christian; it became the essential requirement on everyone's c.v, and the Church began to flourish. Places

of worship were built, money poured in, positions of authority were created, creeds and theologies were formulated, vestments were made of expensive materials and chalices and communion vessels were made of gold and silver and decorated with jewels. Christianity was definitely going places.
But there were some who viewed all this sudden wealth and power with great alarm.

In Egypt, Antony, who several years earlier had been moved by the story of Jesus telling the rich young man to sell all his possessions, had done exactly that. He had given away his possessions and had gone out into the desert to become a hermit. He had been a wealthy, well respected citizen and his actions had taken everyone by surprise. He came to be considered a hero and many young people travelled out into the desert to seek his advice. As a result he was kept informed of what was happening in the world. In around AD 330, the news of the increased wealth and secularisation of the Church began to alarm him and he left the desert and returned to Alexandria to warn the Christian community of the dangers which lay ahead. He was concerned that Christians were forgetting that Christ himself had lived in poverty and had 'nowhere to lay his head'.
Antony was so well respected and his teachings were so compelling that when he returned to the desert so did hundreds of young men, all eager to live in isolation in order to seek the companionship of Christ. For a while the desert caves of Egypt became overcrowded with wildly enthusiastic, young, holy men.

In Gaul, approximately 30 years later, Martin, a young Roman army officer, decided that he, too, must change his life. He had ridden on his horse ahead of his soldiers marching into Amiens. The weather was wet and bitterly cold and he was protected by his large officer's cloak which covered both him and his horse. As he rode into the city he noticed a beggar huddled in a doorway. He was shivering with cold, so Martin got off his horse and, using his sword, he slashed his cloak in half and gave one half to the beggar.
Back at the barracks he was teased by his fellow officers for his actions, but that night he dreamed that Christ came into the barrack rooms wearing the half cloak and proudly saying "See what a fine cloak my friend Martin gave me today." From that day Martin was determined to change his life and to live a life seeking to get to know Christ as his new friend.
Martin's first move was to be baptised but, having been enrolled in the army at the age of 15, he was committed to stay as a soldier for the full 25 years. Finally, in AD 356

and aged 40 he was able to leave to begin his new life. Impressed by stories of Antony he set out to find a desert place where he could live alone as a hermit. He longed for solitude and these first few years alone were to be the happiest in his life. Too soon, the Church, recognising his charismatic leadership skills, decided that he should be fast-tracked through its ranks. In AD 371, obeying orders, as he had done all his life, he was consecrated as Bishop of Tours. This was a reluctant move for Martin and he quickly became known as a different kind of bishop. He had no possessions to move into the Bishop's Palace so, when duties required him to stay there, he would sleep on the floor. He refused to wear vestments or to eat rich foods and, although they found it strange at first, the people learned to love their unusual Bishop. As time went on, however, he gradually began to spend more and more time at a small monastic settlement which he had founded at Marmoutier, and he lived in a little wooden hut which he had built for himself. Most of his young monks were ex-soldiers or sons from wealthy families. Their life at Marmoutier was ones of strict discipline. Martin was training them to go out into the world as evangelist bishops.

In public Martin took every opportunity to preach to the people about the urgent need to look beyond the opulence of the Church, and he encouraged them to seek for themselves a 'desert' place so that they too could spend time alone with Christ.

Martin was not a brilliant preacher; he was often blunt and to the point, but he had a sense of fun and people enjoyed his company. Many travelled long distances to hear him. As a result, young people, in particular, began to follow his advice and sought for themselves a desert place. Some travelled from Britain and returned to set up their own religious foundations. These copied the pattern which Martin had devised, giving each monk an individual, small hut in which to live, in near isolation, and to train them to go out among the people to spread the Gospel. Most of the older church foundations in Britain are dedicated to St Martin and many, like Ninian's church in Whithorn are in their original isolated positions.

Martin died in AD 397. He was 81.

Another 30 years later a British monk named Mawgan, whose Latin name was Pelagius, decided to travel to Rome. His timing was bad. Perhaps being tucked away in his monastery in North Wales he hadn't been aware of what was happening in the world. Perhaps he had no idea of the upheaval of the Germanic tribes and their determination to challenge the armies of Rome. Nevertheless, he went and he eventually arrived in Rome, where the citizens of that city were equally ignorant of the fate which awaited them.

In Rome Pelagius became immediately popular. His kindly demeanour, his love of learning and his down-to-earth, folksy wisdom singled him out as someone to be trusted. He became spiritual director to several important people and the letters he wrote to many of them are still available to us today.

While he was still in Rome, Pelagius was made aware of the teachings of Augustine of Hippo. Augustine was based just across the narrowest point of the Mediterranean Sea in North Africa close to Carthage. His teaching was held in high regard, but Pelagius took issue with many aspects. He accused Augustine of preaching predestination and countered by saying that if mankind was created in the image of God then men must have been given the gift of free choice and must be responsible for their actions. He also argued that when God created mankind He saw that His creation was good and was not soiled by the stigma of 'original sin'.

Pelagius began his criticism of Augustine from a distance but, in AD 409, the threat of invasion by the Visigoths from the north became imminent and Pelagius and many of his new friends fled across the sea to Carthage. In Carthage he met Augustine face to face and, against this seasoned orator, he came off an unfortunate second best. He was excommunicated for his beliefs and, unable to travel in Europe because the whole of Europe was in uproar and travelling was dangerous, he went on to the Holy Land. There he continued his argument with Augustine by letter and managed to get his excommunication lifted for a short while, only to have it re-instated a few years later.

Some say he died in Jerusalem and others that he died in the deserts of Egypt. Either way, he never returned to his native Britain.

Momentous changes were taking place. When the Roman Emperor Theodosius died in AD 395, he had left his eastern empire to his son Arcadius, aged 17, and his western empire to his son Honorius, aged 10. This encouraged the Germanic tribes from northern Europe to begin to move. In AD 406 Vandals, Sueves, Franks and Alans crossed the frozen Rhine and began to ravage Gaul, and, in AD 410, the ancient city of Rome fell to the Visigoths.

Although the Roman capital had been moved to Constantinople 80 years earlier, the loss of Rome was a severe blow to the Empire. Soldiers were recalled from all over Europe to try and keep the invaders back, but to no avail. As a result of their defeat of Rome the Germanic tribes grew in confidence and strength and the Roman empire slowly died. By the end of the century it was no more.

As the invading tribes moved south, the people of Tours had barricaded themselves behind their city walls. They had the body of Martin safe within their church and it filled them with confidence. It was a well founded confidence, because they survived without a scratch, and eventually the invaders settled down and people resumed their lives.

The Church as an institution also survived and, in place of a secular empire, it re-established itself, based in Rome, as the Holy Roman Empire. From AD 476 the known world no longer had an emperor to rule over them. They had a pope.

Antony died in AD 356. Martin died in AD397 and Pelagius died in AD 420.

A hermit, a bishop and a heretic monk. They never met, but their teachings fuelled the spirits of young Christians across Europe at one of the most critical times in history. The scene was set.

Sayings....

ANTONY..

The person who abides in solitude and quiet is delivered from fighting three battles; hearing, speech, and sight. Then there remains one battle to fight – the battle of the heart.

To say that God turns away from the sinful is like saying that the sun hides from the blind.

To read more about Antony. A Life of Antony... Athanasius

MARTIN..

Martin was a man of miracles and action so there are not many pertinent sayings to record. But one is especially telling. Martin died on the bare earth surrounded by grieving parishioners and, hating to see the people so upset, he cried out to God " Father, if your people need me, I will not refuse the work. Your will be done."

To read more about Martin. A life of St. Martin... Sulpitius Severes.
Martin of Tours..The Shaping of Celtic Spirituality.
Christopher Donaldson. Canterbury Press.

PELAGIUS

We have no power to persuade or force people to become disciples. We can only inform them about Jesus, and then let them choose freely whether to follow his example or not.

To read more about Pelagius, The Letters of Pelagius. Celtic Soul Friend. Little Gidding Books.
Pelagius. Life and Letters. B R Rees. Boydell and Brewer Ltd.

CHAPTER TWO

The Celts

In around 700 BC the densely populated region around Salzburg in Austria was invaded, and the settled Celtic tribes, who originated there, were disturbed. Large groups of them dispersed to find new homes. They spoke a Gallic language and had long ancestral connections, and they fled in many directions to find new lands and new grazing for their prized cattle. We find them as far apart as Galatia in northern Turkey, in mainland France and in Britain,

Later it was the turn of the Celtic people, from La Teine in Switzerland. Around 400 BC they too were disturbed by marauding tribes and fled to find new homes. By far the larger number of these La Teine Celtic tribes fled to Britain. Their language was Brithonic and so, when the Romans arrived in AD 34, they decided that the islands should be called 'Britain.' These Celtic people were relatively refined, artistic dreamers but, when full of alcohol, they became fearless warriors. The Gallic Celts, who were already settled in Britain, quickly moved their bases further and further to the north and the west, and the La Teine Celts claimed tribal regions in the mainland to make their own.

As a result it is true to say that present day Ireland and Scotland were settled by the Gallic or Gaelic Celts whereas most of the mainland of England was settled by the Brithonic Celts.

The Celts were a tribal people and each tribe staked its claim on the land and marked its boundaries. There were often skirmishes between the tribes but on the whole, over the next 300 years, the British Isles prospered as a Celtic nation.

Of course they didn't occupy an empty land. The earliest inhabitants of Britain were descendants of the hunters and gatherers who had travelled north from the Mediterranean regions and who had settled in the islands after the ice retreated and the melting waters had separated these islands from mainland France. These people were small and dark haired and kept themselves to themselves. The DNA of many people today, from across most of southern and middle England,Wales and Ireland show links to these early hunters and gatherers and close similarity with the people of southern Spain.

The Celts on the other hand, were taller and stronger. They didn't all have blonde hair but they certainly wished they had. Many of them would dye their darker locks with urine to achieve the desired effect.

Each tribe had its own chief and its own affiliation to a Celtic god. The only thing

which kept the tribes together was the power and the amazing knowledge of the Druids. To become a Druid took many, many years of study. No-one argued with their authority because they had memorised the names and deeds of every family going far back in history. They knew each person and his story. They were the keepers of the secrets. They knew, too, the stories of the various gods. They knew exactly how to make the people behave and would tell them, with great confidence, just what would happen to them if they disobeyed and displeased the gods. They wore their hair and cloaks long and their appearance was often frightening. They were a force to be reckoned with.
There were Druids in Celtic Gaul when Martin became Bishop. When he set up his monastery at Marmoutier he grew his hair long and his fellow Bishops took him to task accusing him of looking like a Druid. But Martin, after 25 years of army life, was done with short hair cuts and took no notice. For the next 300 years Celtic holy men copied his tonsure. They shaved the front of the hair from ear to ear and grew it long at the back. Not the most attractive tonsure, and it makes you wonder if it was ever meant to be a tonsure at all. Perhaps Martin was going bald in the front and left his hair to grow at the back, and his followers just wanted to look like him.

Many of the boundaries of the counties in England today still follow the old Celtic tribal limits, and the names often recall the ancient tribal names. For example, Kent was the home of the Cantii whose god was Epona (pony), the goddess of horses. Still, today, the symbol of Kent, on headed paper and building plaques, is a prancing horse.
When Julius Caesar invaded Kent in 55 BC, the Cantii massed on horseback in their hundreds, and lined the top of the steep, shingle beaches. The Romans were trapped at the bottom of the beach and were petrified by the blood curdling calls of the Celts and by their very weird appearance. Totally naked and covered by a blue woad, they were also smeared with grease and very drunk. Luckily for the Romans, the wind changed and, as they were in danger of losing the boats which had brought them ashore, Caesar ordered them all back to the boats and thence back to the ships. Caesar tried again, and yet again, but met with too many problems and eventually returned to Rome.

These encounters with the Romans had an unusual consequence. The Cantii were so impressed by the plumed helmets of the officers that it wasn't long before a new hair fashion began to appear among them. They took to shaving the sides of their heads

and, allowing the hair from forehead to neck to grow long, they stiffened it with urine into what we might now call a Mohican. Still a British fashion among some, but perhaps not achieved in exactly the same way!
The next time the Romans invaded was during the reign of the Emperor Claudius in AD 43. This time the soldiers had been well prepared and the Cantii didn't stand a chance. Britain (present day England) became part of the Roman Empire and the Celtic tribes slowly became Romanised Britons. For the next 367 years Britain was Roman.

When the Romans invaded they were pagans. Their gods were Jupiter, Neptune and Minerva and a pantheon of their relatives. But the Romans were a superstitious people and were afraid to offend any god, so they generally allowed their conquered people to worship as they wished. Roman and Celtic religious observances existed side by side quite comfortably.
The Roman army, with wives and children and camp followers, settled in Britain around the army bases. The soldiers were of mixed race and came from anywhere in the Roman Empire. They settled and married British women and very soon the country became as one with the countries of the rest of the empire.
Some of the tribes took longer to adopt Roman ways but others, promptly, sued for peace and adapted very quickly.
In the part of Britain to the west of present day Birmingham, the tribe of the Cornovii sued for peace and very soon impressed the Romans with their amazing skill of fighting from horseback. As a result of their exemplary service as a cohort with the regular Roman army along the wall from Newcastle to Carlisle, they were granted civitas status and given the task of clearing out the valleys of Wales where there were still some Gallic Celts holed up and causing trouble. The Cornovii worshipped a serpent shaped god called Cernunus but when, in AD 316 the Roman Empire became Christian they were one of the first of the British tribes to adopt the new religion. Many of them, however, maintained a healthy respect for Cernunus and several legends concerning the Cornovii saints involved a battle with a dragon or serpent.
Until that time, Christianity was considered as just another cult and had existed in Britain as a private religion among some of the Roman families. Christians from noble families would meet for worship in rooms in some of the larger houses and very few independent church buildings have been found which date to this time. The small monastic settlements, set up by the young travelling bishops from Marmoutier,

were generally made of wood or unmortared stone, with small buildings surrounding a central church. Evidence of their existence can sometimes be found under the foundations of some of our oldest churches.

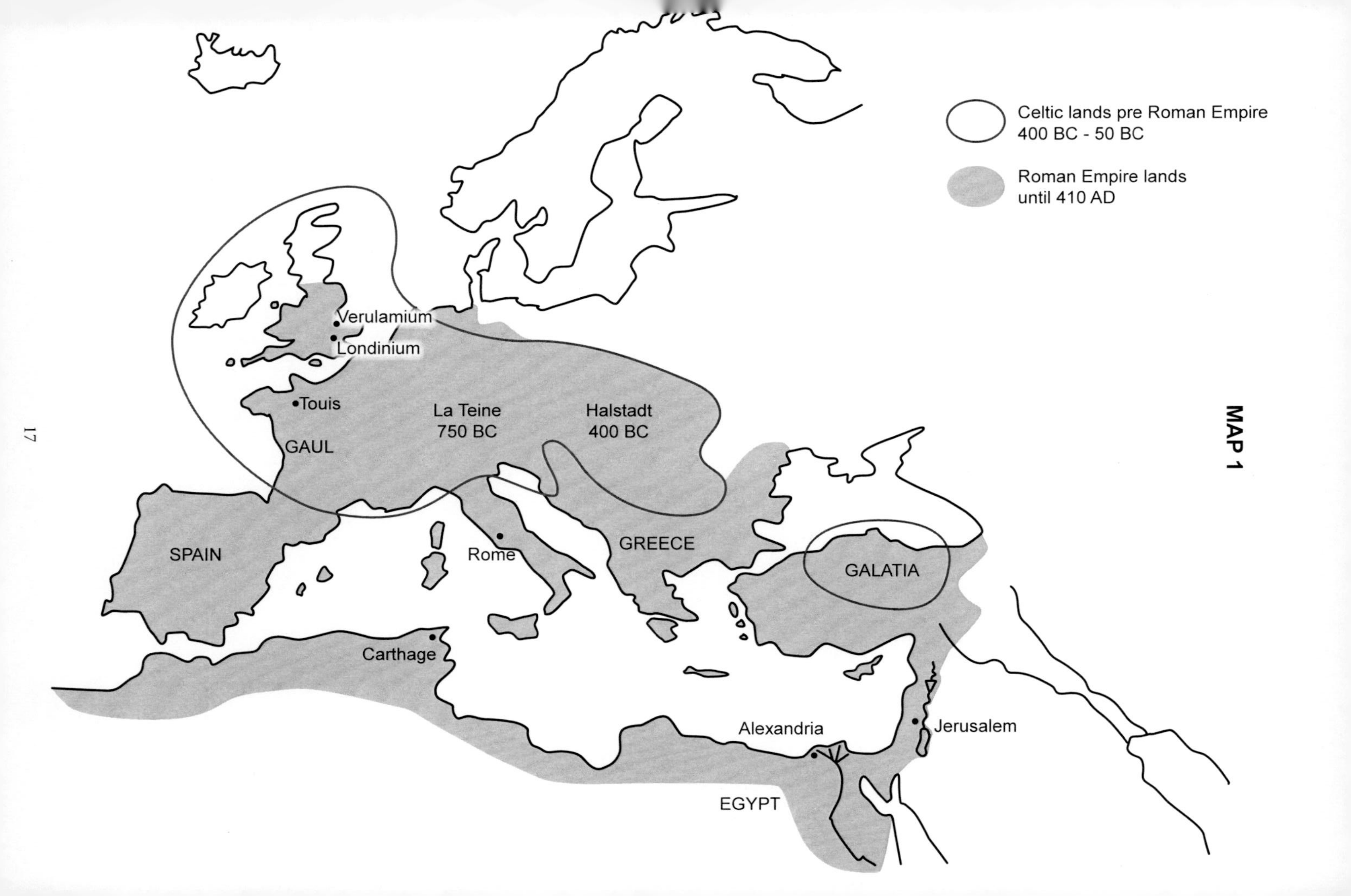
MAP 1
Celtic lands pre Roman Empire
400 BC - 50 BC
Roman Empire lands
until 410 AD
Verulamium
Londinium
Touis
GAUL
La Teine
750 BC
Halstadt
400 BC
SPAIN
Rome
GREECE
GALATIA
Carthage
Alexandria
Jerusalem
EGYPT

The Celtic
Tribes in Britain
MAP 2
Atecotti?
Northern
Picts
Southern
Picts
Damnonii
Votadini
Selgovae
Novantae
Carlisle
Corbridge
Brigantes
Aldborough
York
Ribchester
Parisii
Brough
Lincoln
Chester
Decangi
Ordovices
Wroxeter
Coritani
Leicester
Caistor
Iceni
Cornovii
Catuvellauni
Trinovantes
Colchester
Demetae
Carmarthen
Gloucester
Dobunni
Silures
Caerleon
Cirencester
St Albans
London
Atrebates
Silchester
Winchester
Belgae
Cantium
Canterbury
Dumnonii
Durotriges
Exeter
Dorchester
Chichester
50 mls
80 kms

CHAPTER THREE

Independence

Christians known to us during this period, when Britain was part of a proud Roman Empire, are Alban, Ninian, Patrick and Pelagius. Alban was a citizen of Verulamium who was martyred during the persecution of Christians which took place during the reign of the Emperor Diocletian around AD 305. Ninian was the son of a converted Cumbrian chieftain. As a young man he travelled to Rome and returned via Marmoutier, where he was so impressed by Martin that he founded his own oratory at Whithorn, on the coast in south west Scotland, and, in AD 394, he went on to preach the Gospel to the Picts. Patrick was the son of a Romano British deacon, in Carlisle. Born in AD 389 he was kidnapped as a teenager by Irish invaders and spent six years as a slave in Ireland. He eventually escaped on a boat which was heading for Gaul where he, too, studied and was ordained. When he returned to Britain he decided to go back to Ireland and take the Gospel to the Irish.

In AD 396 Bishop Victricius, Bishop of Rouen and admirer of Martin, visited Britain to talk to the very few British clergy, and to visit Ninian's church and monastic school at Whithorn. It is thought that Victricius may well have been born in Britain himself. He supported Pelagius, and his ideas were much more aligned to the thinking of the British Christians than they ever were to those of the mainstream church in Europe. If the teaching of Pelagius is indicative of the British Christian thought of the time, then it was freer, more open, and the theology was easier to understand. It sprang from common sense rather than from clever, intellectual arguments and it was this fresh approach which appealed to the Roman aristocracy, when Pelagius visited Rome. When Pelagius was excommunicated and went to Egypt, his baton was picked up by an ardent Irish follower named Celestius. Living in Rome, Celestius wrote passionately, defending Pelagian teaching, and was joined by another prolific writer, known to us only as the Sicilian Briton.

These two men gave the Christianity of the day a social conscience. Like Antony, their thinking started with the words of Jesus. " If thou wouldst be perfect, go sell all that thou hast." It continued with the directive that it was a Christian duty to give to the poor. As the Sicilian Briton says,

"Abolish the rich and you will have no more poor... for it is the few rich men who are the cause of the many poor."

Following the reign of Constantine, Britain prospered. The people enjoyed being part of the great Pax Romana, so that when the legions, based in Britain, were recalled to try and save Rome from the Visigoths, it came as a surprise and caused much consternation. The legions were, by then, largely made up of Celtic Britons who had enlisted in the army over the years. In AD 409 the men left for Rome leaving families behind them. No-one knew how long they would be away but no-one doubted that the might of Rome would prevail and they would be back before long. When news eventually reached them of the army's defeat, the whole of Britain despaired. Who would protect them now? The answer, when it came, was 'no-one.' Britain must stand alone.

A group of distinguished elders hastily formed a council and appointed a man, known to us as Vortigern, to be its leader. The name Vortigern means 'First among equals' and may, in fact, have been his title rather than his name, but it gave some credence to the legend that the Council sat at a round table in order that all were indeed equal.. The first and greatest problem the Council had to address was the news that, because of the upheavals in Europe, hordes of displaced people from the continent were beginning to mass on the beaches at Calais, anxious to cross to Britain. Vortigern, and some of the other Council members travelled to Kent to see for themselves, and found that some of the refugees had already landed on the beaches. Vortigern acted quickly and sought out the leader of the group, a Saxon named Hengist, with his son Horsa. Vortigern made an agreement with them there and then. Hengist and Horsa and all their immediate family were welcome to settle in Britain, provided they prevented anyone else from making the crossing.
Payment for these services was agreed and Vortigern and the Council members returned to Londinium, in great relief.
Unfortunately for Vortigern, Hengist saw an opportunity to become wealthy. Making his base on the cliffs of the Isle of Thanet, where he could survey the Channel, he became a human traffiker. Anyone attempting to cross the Channel to enter Britain without paying large sums of money up front, was severely dealt with. Only those who could find the money were allowed to cross. Gradually large numbers of Angles, Saxons and Jutes, desperate to find a new, safer place to live, began arriving in Britain. They crossed in long boats, mostly at night, and made for river estuaries so that their boats could take them, often several miles in land, before they needed to disembark. Armed only with long, thin knives and accompanied by their families and children, they were anxious and desperate. And this desperation made them dangerous.

By the time Vortigern got to hear of the vast numbers which were invading in this way, it was already too late. He rushed to Kent again and Hengist wined and dined him and told him that the task was too great for his small family, and he needed more members of his own Saxon tribe to help him. At the table was Hengist's daughter and Vortigern was distracted. She was very beautiful and, a very drunk Vortigern fell helplessly in love. As a result Vortigern agreed to allow more Saxons to enter Britain, and to be on the payroll of the Council. He also agreed to hand over Kent to the immigrants. In return Vortigern took Hengist's daughter as his wife.

On return to Londinium his fellow Council members were furious. They refused to pay any more to the Saxons, saying that Vortigern had let them down. The leader of the opposition was a Council member called Ambrosius Aurelianus, an elderly statesman descended from the Roman aristocracy, and he was backed by wealthy families who refused to donate any more money. The promised wages were cut short, and the contract was broken, so the Saxons rebelled and rampaged through the countryside, burning everything that would burn. The wealthy, noble British families began to panic. Fearing for their lives, they hastily packed their treasured possessions into wagons and, accompanied by their families, servants and slaves, they started heading west.

With his plan in shatters, Vortigern decided that the Council should also head west and he hastily moved Britain's capital from Londinium to Gloucester and made a protective barrier across Britain from York to Dorset, roughly following an original old Roman defensive boundary.

Over the next 50 years more and more British families fled west as the invaders continued to cross the channel. The Britons became refugees in their own country. It was those who could afford wagons to carry their possessions who made the journey. The poorer members of the population hunkered down and stayed where they were, allowing the invaders to settle among them.

With British soldiers patrolling the new defensive border, Vortigern and the Council abandoned the east of Britain to the invaders and deployed the Cornovii to the far south west with instructions to keep the southern coast free from Saxon invaders, and the north coast free of the Irish. The Cornovii were also to assist the wealthy Britons by keeping all routes south open and safe for the travellers.

Many of the fleeing Britons found sanctuary in the valleys of Powys which had been successfully cleared of the Gallic Celts by the Cornovii. Others travelled further and went to the south west corner of Britain and paid for boats to take them to safety in the far north west of France. Travelling with the wealthiest of these British families were family retained doctors, teachers and Christian priests. When they found new lands to make their homes, the teachers and priests were encouraged to set up small schools so that the children of the family and the children of the neighbours could be educated and grow up to be well versed in the classics and in Christian studies. Many of the priests and teachers had been influenced by Martin. Some had even trained at Marmoutier. This was their moment. Cut off from the wealthy Roman Church, and with no-one to tell them otherwise, they had the chance to change things!

CHAPTER FOUR

The teachers come into their own

People elected to positions of power in either Church or State should think twice before messing with teachers. A teacher's influence can do either great good or great harm. It might take time, but a malleable child will, one day, grow to become a mover and shaker of the future.

And so it came to pass. In the new homesteads of the refugee British families, in the valleys of the west, the teachers taught and imparted radical, new Christian ideals. Following both Antony and Martin, they taught the importance of the individual journey of the soul and how necessary it was to seek the solitude the soul needed to become close to Christ. Following Martin, they taught how important it was to care for the stranger and to see in him the embodiment of Christ and, following Pelagius, they taught their young pupils to keep their theology simple and to look to the people around them, to nature and all living things in order to seek God and listen to His voice.

The grand buildings, with their decorated Christian meeting rooms, had been left behind. There were no churches and no church organisation. These wealthy families had to start all over again. The teachers had free reign.

They taught that Nature itself was the only temple they needed for their worship of God, and Christ was the only companion they needed for their journey. Despite the obvious wealth of their sponsors, the teachers taught that wealth and power were at odds with a Christ who walked this earth in poverty and therefore should either be shunned or used only for the glory of God..

Another aspect of their teaching, which was to take on great importance, concerned the Holy Spirit. The great, ever moving power of the Spirit thrilled them and gave them confidence and strength. This does not appear to be so important to the Church they left behind, so perhaps it was the exodus from their previous homes and the flight across England which made them aware of the Spirit of God guiding and directing their lives. Seeing God as Father, Son and Holy Spirit, with a threefold power, gave

both confidence and excitement to their lives.
The teachers, like Martin at Marmoutier, expected absolute discipline. They used the scriptures, and particularly the Gospel of St Joh,n to teach the word of God, and they expected their pupils to learn all the psalms by heart. They may have been strict, but they were inspiring, and a pupil was more likely to discipline himself in disappointment at letting his teachers down rather than be disciplined by them. For this reason each young pupil was given an older buddy to be his counsellor, or soul friend, whose job it was to make sure that the pupil was not too hard on himself.
Some of the teachers proved to be so good that pupils came to them from long distances and had to live in small huts or barns in the grounds. These schools became quite famous and Illtyd in Lantwit Major in South Wales, Petroc in Cornwall, Carantoc in Southern Ireland, Budoc in Brittany, Columba in Iona, Cuby in Anglesey and Aidan in Lindisfarne are all remembered as being exceptional teachers of the faith.

As had been the fashion at Marmoutier, when schooling was finished and the young people reached adulthood, they were encouraged to adopt a Christian martyrdom. For those who were the eldest in the family and who would, one day, take on their father's responsibilities, there was the red martyrdom. These young men would often spend time with other families and train to be squires, or join the army, before returning to care for the family estate. Their pledge was to fight to the death if necessary to protect their families and the Christian faith. This martyrdom was also adopted by younger sons who had no aptitude for learning and who enjoyed a more physical life.
Those of the young men who longed to travel and take the message of Christ out into the world would adopt the white martyrdom. They often stayed longer with the teachers and only left when the teachers felt they were ready and, even then, they were generally sent out in groups, so that they could travel together. The leader of the group would be presented with a piece of slate marked with five small crosses. This was to be his travelling altar and would mark the foundation of the group's first church. Once the foundation church had been established, the leader of the group would present each of his companions, in turn, with their own portable altar, and send them out to found their own churches. These were all generally quite close to each other so that the young men could keep in touch with each other.
We also hear of stories which tell us that young women were attending some of these schools in Wales and in Ireland and that they, too, chose to travel with the men. Many of these young women set up nunneries near river or road crossings where

they welcomed travellers and cared for them. These were places of quiet refreshment and were regularly used by the travelling saints and refugee Christian families

The last martyrdom was the green martyrdom which was adopted by those who wanted to live a simple, solitary life of prayer. Once a quiet deserted place was found these young men and women rarely moved and settled there for life. Their's was the life of a hermit. They, too, had their followers among local people who saw them as being both wise and holy and who would come to them in times of need.

One thing these early teachers and priests were very strict about was the Eucharist. It would seem that this service followed, to the word, the exact pattern of the Church in Rome and we can see, in the poetry of these young men and women, just how much it meant to them. Interestingly, chalices from this time seem to have been much larger, with two sturdy handles, which probably indicates that they were passed around rather than offered individually.

When the white martyrs travelled, as well as their portable altar, they carried with them a chalice and a plate, a white linen cloth, a candle, a bell and a staff. In a leather satchel they carried a copy of St John's Gospel and any other books they had the privilege of owning. And when they left their homes and schools behind, they stepped out into the world, accompanied by their friends and full of excitement for where the Spirit would lead them.

As time passed and families became established in the north and west of England, the displaced Britons began to feel secure in their new homes. More and more British families continued to trek west and join them until a great network of these wealthy families stretched from the far north, through Wales and the West Country, all the way to Brittany, which took its name from these British refugees.

The Saxons tried to move further west but were regularly repulsed by an enthusiastic British army. It was an exciting time to be young and the children of these noble and wealthy families grew up eager to prove themselves worthy of their chosen martyrdom.

Celtic Christianity may have had its roots in the dreams of inspired teachers from the past, but it is in the deeds and words of the enthusiastic, young missionaries, who had chosen the white martyrdom, that it came to fruition. Known as Sancta Peregini, or 'Pilgrim Saints' they left home and, in the name of Christ, they travelled the Western world to spread the Gospel. They knew there were family friends with whom they could keep in touch along the way, but there were many unknown dangers still to face, and when they left home they had no way of knowing whether they would see their parents again. Finding somewhere safe to sleep at night was a serious problem

but, as they travelled in groups, there was a certain safety in numbers.
Each morning, before they left to face the day they would use binding prayers as they dressed and laced their shirts, boots and trousers securely around them. Then they would stand and face the rising sun and, raising a hand and turning their bodies in a clockwise direction, they would draw three circles in the air and invoke the protection of God the Father, God the Son and God the Holy Spirit. Having thus drawn a Caim (pronounced Cyme), or threefold protective force field, around themselves, they were then ready to go out into the world to face whatever the day had in store for them.

St Ninian's Catechism.

Question. What is best in this world?
Answer. To do the will of our Maker
Question. What is his will?
Answer. That we should live according to the laws of his creation.
Question. How do we know these laws?
Answer. By study – studying the scriptures with devotion.
Question. What tool has our Maker provided for this study.
Answer. The intellect, which can probe everything.
Question. And what is the fruit of study.
Answer. To perceive the eternal word of God reflected in every plant and insect, every bird and animal, and every man and woman.

A Hermit's Prayer.

Grant me, sweet Christ, the grace to find, Son of the living God
A small hut in a lonesome spot
To make it my abode.

A little pool, but very clear, to stand beside the place,
Where every sin is washed away
By sanctifying grace.

A pleasant woodland all about, to shield it from the wind
And make a home for singing birds
Before it and behind.

A southerm aspect for the heat, a stream along its foot
A smooth green lawn, with rich topsoil
Propitious for all fruit.

A lovely church, a home for God, bedecked with linen fine
Where'oer the whitened Gospel page
The Gospel candle shines.

Abbot Monteith. 6th Century.

A Binding Prayer, (Part of 'St. Patrick's Breastplate.'
I bind unto myself today
The power of God to hold and lead
His eye to watch, His might to stay,
His ear to hearken to my need.
The wisdom of my God to teach,
His hand to guide, His shield to ward;
The word of God to give me speech,
His heavenly host to be my guard.

A Simple Caim.
May God the Father protect me and keep me safe.
May God the Son comfort me and walk with me along the way.
May God the Holy Spirit keep me strong and fill my heart with courage.
May God the Holy Trinity bless me now. Amen

MAP 3

Britain during
5th Century AD
ALBA
(Scotland)
Lindisfarne
Iona
NORTHUMBERLAND
Whithorn
Hadrian's
Wall
Derry
Bangor
Carlisle
Whitby
Armagh
CUMBRIA
York
Tara
Kildare
Anglesey
LINE
Lincoln
Chester
DEFENCE
Wroxeter
Norwich
BRITISH
Verulamium
CYMRI
Carmarthen
Gloucester
Caerleon
Londinium
Thanet
Llantwit Major
Salisbury
Canterbury
Winchester
Ilchester
Portsmouth
Tintagel
Dorchester
Exeter
Castle
Dor
Hayle
British Refugees
Angle, Saxon &
Jutish invaders

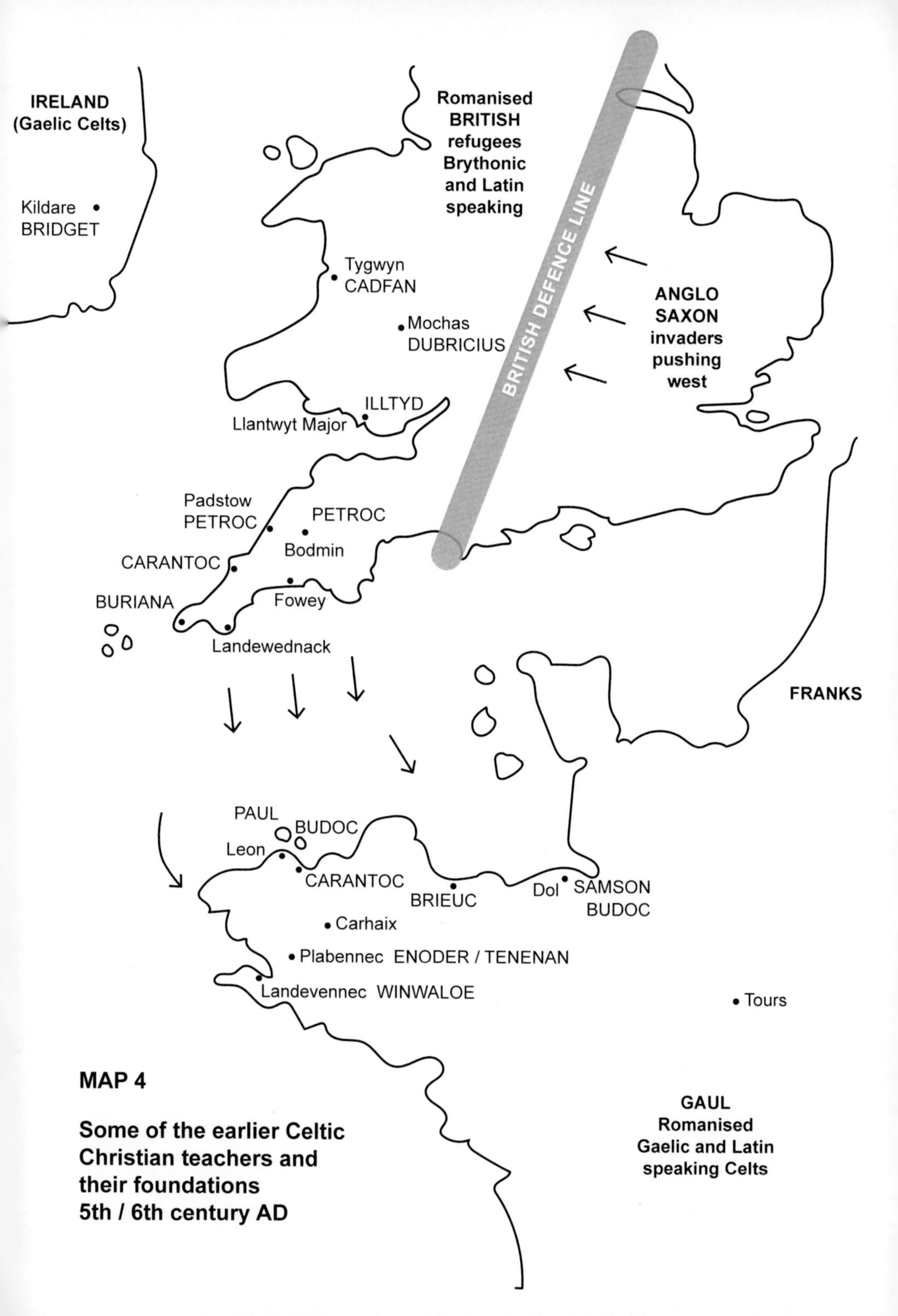
IRELAND
(Gaelic Celts)
Kildare
BRIDGET
Romanised
BRITISH
refugees
Brythonic
and Latin
speaking
BRITISH DEFENCE LINE
Tygwyn
CADFAN
Mochas
DUBRICIUS
ANGLO
SAXON
invaders
pushing
west
ILLTYD
Llantwyt Major
Padstow
PETROC
PETROC
Bodmin
CARANTOC
BURIANA
Fowey
Landewednack
FRANKS
PAUL
BUDOC
Leon
CARANTOC
BRIEUC
Dol
SAMSON
BUDOC
Carhaix
Plabennec ENODER / TENENAN
Landevennec WINWALOE
Tours
MAP 4
Some of the earlier Celtic
Christian teachers and
their foundations
5th / 6th century AD
GAUL
Romanised
Gaelic and Latin
speaking Celts

CHAPTER FIVE

Britain in trouble

Germanus

Back in Gloucester, Vortigern struggled to maintain his position of power. Finances had all but dried up and the soldiers along the defensive line still had to be paid and supported. Ambrosius Aurelianus, with the support of many other nobles, had formed his own private army of soldiers who were better equipped than Vortigern's soldiers and who made adventurous and heroic sorties against the Saxons. Vortigern's soldiers began to feel demoralised and Vortigern himself had lost the confidence of Council members. It was an impossible position for Vortigern, and he sank into a depression and began to drink heavily. Legend says that he had an incestuous relationship with his daughter who gave birth to a son, Faustus.

To add to his miseries, Bishop Germanus had arrived by ship from Gaul with the express purpose of stamping out what was now called the Pelagian heresy. The British Christians, in the west, closed ranks and Germanus had very little success, but he discovered that Vortigern had fathered a child by his daughter and he was horrified. He stood outside Vortigern's residence and prayed and fasted for 40 days and 40 nights, insisting that Vortigern must repent.

The year was AD 446 and, just when Vortigern felt that his situation could not get worse, Hengist, unexpectedly, sent a message to Vortigern suggesting that the time had come for the British and the Saxons to form a new contract based on peace and perpetual friendship. Vortigern hastily called the Council together and on their advice he accepted Hengist's proposals.

A delighted Hengist immediately called for a feast and entertainment to ratify the treaty and invited Vortigern, the British nobles and the military officers to attend. 300 of the British aristocracy turned up for the feast and Vortigern was once again back in favour. Briefly.

Hengist was a welcoming host and the 300 British guests were equally matched by 300 Saxons who mingled, in a friendly manner, among the British so that when they sat down to eat, each sat next to a British guest. When the British were sufficiently inebriated, Hengist suddenly stood up and shouted, 'Saxons, draw your knives!' and immediately each Saxon reached into his boot where his long knife had been concealed, and plunged it into the body of the Briton sitting next to him. The only

Briton to survive this massacre was Vortigern, and he only escaped with his life by signing over the counties of Essex, Middlesex and Sussex to Hengist. All the British Council members died that day, including Ambrosius Aurelianus, and a large number of the trusted and experienced army officers. Vortigern and his wives fled. They took refuge in an old castle which was struck by lightning and caught fire. His wives died, but Vortigern survived yet again. It is said he eventually died a sad and lonely death, in a ditch, close to the Welsh coast.
Germanus returned to Gaul, taking with him Vortigern's young son, Faustus, who was brought up and educated by Germanus and who, eventually, built a monastery on the banks of the river Renis.

In Nennius' History of the Britons, written in the 8th century, he seems to indicate that it was at this point that Arthur stepped into the breach. Most historians, however, question this and believe that it was Ambrosius Aurelianus' son, Ambrosius Aurelianus II, who took control. He unified the army and, while the Saxons poured across the channel and swarmed over the British countryside, and assisted by able, young officers, he rebuilt the defences and organised the resistance so that the British families in their new settlements began to feel safe once more. The Saxons spread into the areas lost by Vortigern but the old barrier was still manned by British soldiers. It was a barrier which said, 'so far, but no further'. More British families from mainland Britain still trekked west and, as they left, the Saxons divided up their deserted villas and extensive lands. Again some of the families settled in the West Country but even more fled to Brittany.

Whether Ambrosius died in battle or simply retired we don't know but there followed approximately 35 years of peace while the Saxons consolidated their position and began to farm their new lands. At some time during this period, possibly byAD 475, Ambrosius had been succeeded by Arthur. This short window marks the period during which the young men and women who had been schooled in Wales began to embark on their missionary journeys.
Arthur was a Christian. He wore the red cross of martyrdom on his breastplate and, on one occasion, he is even recorded as carrying an image of the Virgin Mary with Child, on his arm. Artorius is a Roman family name, so, like Ambrosius, he, too, was descended from a distinguished Roman family. There are many legends about Arthur, but it would seem that, as in the time of Vortigern, his Council still sat around a round table and his Knights were all drawn from among the remaining British noble

families. The most important event during his time was the battle of Badon in AD 495, when the British soundly defeated the Saxon invaders and there followed a long period of peace.

During the years which followed the death of the British nobles at the conference on the 'night of the long knives', more and more British refugees left their homes to flee north and west. From the western parts of Northumberland, Cumbria, Wales (Cymry), Somerset, Devon, Cornwall and across the sea in Brittany, the British families formed themselves into a brotherhood. Encouraged by Ambrosius and Arthur, it became a network of support and loyalty. Although many still spoke and wrote in Latin, as time went on it was the Brithonic tongue which came to the fore. The name Cymry or Cumber means brotherhood, and the old motto of Cornwall, 'One and all', reflects the close bond between the families. Alone they could not survive, but together they had a chance. They were fiercely Christian and the Christianity they now held dear was the Christianity of Martin, Antony and Pelagius. They were proud of the quality of their Christian teachers, known in Latin as 'doctors' and they actively sought out the best of them to teach their children. The homesteads which could boast a chapel and a teacher were known as Lans or Llans. In Wales and Cornwall the teacher's names were often linked, as time went on, with the 'doc' 'toc' and 'roc' of doctor. For example Budoc, Carantoc, Petroc. All famous teachers.
The word Welsh and Wales is a Saxon word meaning 'foreigners' and is obviously not what the Cymry called themselves. In the same way 'Cornwall' was to the Saxons 'the land of the Cornovii foreigners.'
During the latter period of the reign of Ambrosius and for almost all of the reign of Arthur, the British families felt reasonably safe. Most of the families in Britain had relatives who had crossed the Channel and who had settled in N W France, giving the region the name of Brittany (Little Britain) and, the young people, in particular, made frequent crossings, keeping the families in touch. Devon and Cornwall did not attract many settlers but were seen more as land bridges connecting the families in the Welsh valleys with those in Brittany. Both Devon and Cornwall were crossed and recrossed many times, especially by the young missionaries who had adopted the White martyrdom. Both counties today have white crosses on their flags in honour of these young saints and almost every village or town in Cornwall, is dedicated to the memory of one of the missionaries or hermits from this period.

Using the Lives of the Saints, mostly written during the 9th century and as interpreted by Canon Doble, we will look at some of the stories which have been recorded, starting with the stories concerning the royal families of the Britons in Cornwall, or, as it was then known, ' Dumnonia'

CHAPTER SIX

The Cornish royal family

Conomorus was a warlord who ruled over extensive lands in southern Cornwall and also in western Brittany, around the town of Carhaix, during the 6th century. His court was at Lantyan and Castle Dore, the old Bronze Age fortification on the hill above Fowey. Interestingly, the castle and village of Carhayes, on his lands in Cornwall, although spelled differently, bear the same name as his town in Brittany. Conomorus spent a great deal of his time travelling by sea between his two kingdoms. In Britonnic his name Conomorus means 'Hound of the Sea.'

It is extremely likely that Conomorus was one of the Cornovii officers sent by Vortigern to settle in the area and repel Saxon invaders. His name, the position of his residences and his eagerness to acquire more and more lands, all seem to point to a Cornovii background. It is from families such as his that Cornwall eventually got its name, 'The land of the Cornovii Welsh'. In the 'life' of his great grandson, Cybi, there is a family tree which calls Conomorus a 'military chieftan' rather than 'king', which I think is a very fitting description. His dates and the list and order of his family members are different in every known source, so I have chosen to follow the story which was considered to be most accurate by Canon Gilbert Doble.

Conomorus was also known by the Christian name of Mark. The Cornovii had become a Christian tribe and Conomorus wanted his family and the people of his kingdoms to be schooled in this new religion and needed someone to teach them. He wrote to the now famous, Illtyd, at his school in Llantwit Major in South Wales asking him to send some of his young students to bring the Gospel to Dumnonia. Illtyd agreed and sent 12 young men led by a young student called Paul Aurelianus, a descendant of the illustrious family of which Ambrosius was a member and whose 'life' was written by a monk called Wromonoc.

The young missionaries worked hard in the Fowey area, evangelising the community and tutoring the wives and children of Conomorus. They stayed for 6 years and then, handing over their new church foundations to trusted church members, they asked permission to leave in order to move on to Brittany. How committed to the new faith Conomorus was is debatable, but he was very reluctant to let Paul go as he wanted him to remain in the area as his bishop. It was early days and the new 'kings' or 'war lords' were trying to set themselves up as legitimate leaders. To turn his lands into a diocese, and have a tame bishop, would be a real feather in Conomorus' hat. But Paul was adamant. He needed to go in search of his 'desert' place. West Britain was becoming far too crowded and so Conomorus was very reluctantly persuaded, and Paul and his companions left his court.

The young men walked down to Newlyn to find a boat to take them across the Channel but discovered that they had arrived too late in the year and that the boats would not be crossing the Channel until the winter storms were over. Paul's sister, Sitafolia, had a small nunnery next to Gwavas lake, situated in the woods which skirted the shore near Newlyn. She was concerned that the sea level was rising and she was anxious that it was encroaching on her buildings. When Paul saw the situation he was concerned for his sister and he and his disciples spent the winter moving her and her companions to a new building on the cliffs. They were right to be worried because, within a few years, the woodland and the old buildings were under water. Now the only reference to the land and the lake which was once there, can be found on maritime charts. The lower stumps of the trees of the forest which once covered the area between Newlyn and St Michael's Mount can still be seen at exceptionally low tides each year. And it is interesting that, in the earliest annals of the area, St Michael's Mount is referred to as, 'The Hoar Rock in the Forest'.
The Church of Paul Aurelian, or St Pol de Leon, still marks the place of Sitafolia's new nunnery in the village of Paul on the cliffs between Newlyn and Mousehole. It is a lovely old church, in excellent condition, and much loved by the people of the area. It is well worth a visit.

Paul and his disciples went on to Brittany where Paul was determined to find a' desert' place where he could spend the rest of his life. He visited Count Withures (Victor), a cousin who had settled in the region close to the ancient town of Leon, at the time of the first migration. Withures owned a great deal of land and he gifted Paul the Isle of Batz, or Battha, to be his hermitage. This was all Paul wanted. He had found what he had been searching for, and he was supremely happy. According to his life story, written by Wrmonoc circa.AD 880, he spent long periods alone and when he did venture into the villages he performed several healing miracles and led a 120 foot serpent out of a nearby cave and sent it on his way. (Miracles of this kind were often included to impress the reader.) Withures, however, was so impressed by his cousin with his piety and his wonderful spiritual gifts that he urged him to become a bishop and form a diocese in Withures' extensive lands. Yet again Paul refused, but his cousin didn't give up and, in the end, he tricked Paul into taking an important letter to the king in Paris. Unbeknown to Paul, the letter he carried from Withures told the king of Paul's miraculous gifts and urged him to insist that Paul be consecrated as a Bishop. The king agreed and three other bishops were brought forward to consecrate Paul as Bishop of a new Diocese of Leon which would be sponsored by the wealth of his cousin.

When he returned to Leon, Paul juggled his duties as Bishop with his determination to remain a hermit, and, working to the very end, he lived until he was 104. Paul knew before he died that the people of his island and the people of Leon would argue about where his body should lie, so he gave careful instructions as to what should happen. His body was put in a coffin and the coffin was laid across the backs of two equal wagons which had been parked back to back, one facing the island and one facing the town. Half of the coffin was on one wagon and the other half was on the other. The wagon drivers moved away from each other at the same time and the coffin stayed balanced on the one going to the town, and was greeted with much joy as it entered in through the gates. The saint had chosen his resting place.

While Paul was fulfilling his martyrdom in Brittany, back in Cornwall, Conomorus was living an entirely different life. He had married three wives in contracts designed to increase his lands and influence, and we know the names of four of his children: Iudual (Lud), Tristan, Constantine and Crida.

Conomorus became heavily involved in politics . He was constantly on the look out for new allies and new ways of enlarging his wealth. At one time he was keen to make friends with the Irish. Plans were made for him to marry Isolde, the young daughter of an Irish king and he sent his son Tristan to Ireland, to bring her back to Cornwall. On the long journey back, Tristan and Isolde fell in love and, when they arrived at Castle Dore and Tristan spoke to his father about his feelings, Conomorus flew into a rage and banished Tristan from Britain. Tristan crossed the Channel and settled in France and eventually married a French girl, also named Isolde. When she heard about Tristan's marriage Isolde, in Fowey, was inconsolable and killed herself, and, when Tristan heard of her death he, too, committed suicide.

On the hill behind the town of Fowey, close to Castle Dore, is a large standing stone which tells us that 'Drustanus (Tristan) son of King Mark lies here.'

The only thing we know about Lud, Conomorus' eldest son, is that he was the father of Geraint whose name is remembered further along the coast at Gerrans. Of this Constantine we know nothing but there are legends about Crida that are worth exploring.

Crida longed to give her life to Christ and begged her father to let her leave home

and travel with the young saints from South Wales. Conomorus refused, but did eventually agree that she could set up a monastery somewhere on his own land. A sunny, sheltered spot on the east shore of the River Fal, was chosen. Across the narrow river was the old Roman fort of Golden and boats were coming and going all the time. Crida set up her nunnery and made it a place of refuge and peace for travellers leaving for, or arriving from, Brittany. She is said to have told her nuns that when they prayed they should stand or kneel in a different place each day, because, when they prayed, Christ himself would stand by their side and his footprints would make each spot holy.
Throughout his life, her father continued trying to expand both his kingdom and his wealth, but he eventually made a serious mistake and backed the wrong contender in a struggle for power in Brittany. He and his men were chased back towards Carhaix. Conomorus was wounded and fell from his horse and was trampled to death. His body was recovered and taken back to be buried in Castle Dore.

Conomorus' eldest son, Lud, may have been in Brittany with his father. We have no stories of him succeeding his father at Castle Dore, but it is likely that he did. Lud's son, Geraint (Gerontius), however, had already established himself on the next land promontory which juts out into the Channel at a place now called Gerrans. This must have happened on the instructions of his grandfather while he was still alive. Perhaps, as early as possible, Conomorus encouraged his sons and grandsons to take on kingly duties and the responsibility of guarding the coast from invaders, as it freed him up to spend more time in Brittany where he believed the opportunities were far greater. Geraint must also have been quite young, but we are told that he was a personable and friendly young man and quickly made a name for himself with his generous hospitality. He is also recorded as being a member of Arthur's Round Table.
Geraint and his wife Enid had one son, Erbin (Ervan), who contracted polio when still a toddler. There was news of an Irish, Christian, holy woman who had the gift of healing and who lived at the far end of Cornwall, in Penwith. Her name was Beriana. Erbin was put in a cart and the family took him to Beriana, where he was miraculously healed.
There is a legend in which Geraint, as a young father, answered a call to arms from Arthur and joined the British army on a sortie to prevent Saxons landing at Portsmouth. Unfortunately Geraint was killed, and the death of this brave and lovely young man shocked the British people who lamented the loss of 'the flower of British youth.'

When Geraint's son, Erbin (Ervan), became head of the family at Gerrans, his great, grandfather Conomorus may still have been alive.. We are not sure how old Erbin was when he became king but he reigned in mid Cornwall for the next 30 years.
One of the first things he did when he became king was to build a chapel in honour of Beriana, the saint who had healed him. It was built on the site of the present church in the village of Veryan. (Bs and Vs were interchangeable letters then, as were Gs and Ws.)
Erbin was a steady, popular king and the people prospered under his care. He continued his family's growing dedication to Christianity and was known to be compassionate and generous. He had four boys: Constantine, Selevan, Yestin and Cynga. He is remembered at St. Ervan's church near Padstow and, possibly, at St Erme, near Truro. King Arthur died at Camlann sometime during Erbin's reign in the year AD 515.
When Erbin died he was succeeded by Constantine, who had already established his court on the western side of the mouth of the River Fal. Constantine started his reign quite aggressively and was more like his great, great, grandfather, Conomorus, than his gentle father Erbin. His behaviour caused the historian Gildas to rebuke him soundly as 'a horrid abomination.' At this time, the only person who saw Constantine's gentle side was his beloved wife, another Enid.
Constantine enjoyed hunting and his favourite hunting ground was the Goss Moor near Castle an Dynas. On one occasion his men had cornered a deer and had sent for him to come and finish it off, but the Christian holy man Petroc appeared, and the deer hid behind him. Constantine arrived and angrily ordered Petroc to get out of the way. Petroc continued to shield the deer and he pointed his hand at Constantine and ordered him to stay where he was. To his horror, Constantine found he could not move. Taking advantage of his captive, Petroc proceeded to preach to Constantine, spelling out his faults and reminding him again of his Christian duties. When Petroc released the King, Constantine returned home a chastened man. And later, when his wife Enid died, he abdicated and went to join a monastery. Years later, he died on a mission in the western isles of Scotland.
Constantine's abdication caused a problem. He had no sons and his brother, Selevan, had become a hermit and was living on the cliffs in West Penwith. His second brother, Yestin (Just), had become a hermit and was living by the sea close by at the mouth of the Roseland peninsular, and the other brother, Cynga, was not at all interested in taking on the throne. The only male member of the family that was left was Selevan's son Cybi (Cuby), and Cybi also refused the throne and, taking with him uncle Cynga

and a small group of Cornish enthusiasts, he declared that he was going to Ireland. Cybi's adventures with his wild Cornish companions are quite amusing, but possibly not to those they met on the way. His Cornish companions were argumentative and a bit thoughtless and upset people everywhere they landed and tried to settle. They were constantly being told to move on. Nobody wanted them, but, finally, they were allowed to settle on a rocky outcrop on the Isle of Anglessey, where the disciples had to grow up if they wanted to survive. Eventually Cybi was able to establish a centre of learning in this inhospitable place which was recognised all over the Celtic world. The stories of the Conomorus family are difficult to date exactly without knowing, for sure, just how long each member lived. Conomorus himself is said to have died in AD 560, but at what age? Paul Aurelanius is said to have died at the age of 104, but in what year? It is possible that Paul was still alive in Brittany when Constantine abdicated, but that possibility is very uncertain. A very old man when he died, he may have followed news of the Conomorus family with great interest, or he may never have known that his influence on the family, all those years before, had finally come to fruition. One by one, each of them had rejected wealth and power and had turned to Christ.

CHAPTER SEVEN

Patrick and Carantoc

Patrick was born around the year AD 386, in Bannavern, which is thought to have been near Carlisle.. The Romans had been in Britain for over 300 years and his father, Calpurnius, was employed, in some way, by the army and was also a deacon in the Christian Church. His mother, Conchessa, was related to Martin in Tours. When he was 16, Patrick was captured by Irish invaders and taken to Ballymeena in Antrim where he was kept as a slave for six, hard, years.

His job was to look after pigs, and he was often cold and wet and hungry. In his 'confessio' written when he was an old man, he says that this was the time of his life when he really learned about prayer.

After six years, he managed to escape by hiding on a boat carrying wolfhounds to Gaul and, once there, he managed to contact his mother's family. He studied for three years at a monastery in Lerins and then went to Auxerre where he was ordained deacon. In AD 431 he was sent to assist a bishop, known as Palladius, who was attempting to evangelise the Irish in Wicklow. Palladius had established three churches but he was worn out and, within a year of Patrick's arrival, he went on to Scotland. In AD 432 bishop Germanus of Auxerre consecrated Patrick as bishop in charge of the evangelising of all Ireland.

The first church foundation Patrick created was at Satal Patraic, and then, realising he stood no chance of making any real progress in Ireland without the backing of the High King, he went to see King Laoghaire in Tara. It was the eve of Beltane and a great bonfire had been built on the hill outside the town. The people were all in their homes waiting for the moment when the fires were ceremonially lit by the Druids and when everyone was called to the fire for the ritual celebrations.

Determined to make sure that Laoghaire paid attention to him, Patrick decided to light the fire himself. All of a sudden the sky lit up with the light of the fire. Everyone was shocked. It was obviously too early for the ceremony which took place at midnight. The King and the Druid priests were furious. After letting it be known that he had been responsible, Patrick hid. He had challenged the Druids and they desperately needed to find him and punish him if they were not to lose face in front of the people. But Patrick remained hidden until the Druids gave up looking and then he suddenly appeared in Laoghaire's court and demanded an audience with the King.

Despite himself, Laoghaire was impressed by this holy man. His quiet presence and his obvious intelligence gave him an air of authority and, when Patrick asked leave to establish schools and churches in the area, Laoghaire agreed and even asked if he could receive instruction himself.

Patrick established many churches and set up several schools, but, all the while, he was nervous of the Druids who were determined to get their own back. Patrick found that the only way he could go about his daily tasks was to invoke the power of the Trinity to protect him. St Patrick's Breastplate

was discovered in his 'Confessio' and gives us a glimpse of his prayers at the time. And, as the Christianity which Patrick had brought to Ireland gradually spread throughout the country, so the power of the Druids diminished and eventually died out.

In AD 442 Patrick visited Rome and talked to Pope Leo of his work in Ireland. The Pope was anxious that the Church in Ireland should not be infected by the Pelagianism of the rebellious British Church in western Britain and the two men agreed that Ireland should be directly subordinate to Rome and entirely independent of Britain. The fact that merchant ships had continued their trading operations between the Mediterranean countries, Cornwall and Ireland, by skirting around the disturbances of mainland Europe, and the fact that travelling through war torn Britain was so dangerous, meant that direct contact with Rome was the only sensible option.

When he returned from Rome, Patrick established the cathedral church of Armagh and made it the educational and administrative centre of the Irish Church.

Patrick died in AD 461 but only after he made a pact with God. In a vision he discussed with God his biggest worry. He was afraid that no-one would understand and love the argumentative Irish as he did, so he made God promise that when an Irish man died, he, and not Peter, would be at the gates of Heaven to say 'yea' or 'nay' to his entry!

He died at Saul, on Strangford Lough in Down Patrick, and it is because we have his story, his poems and his prayers, written in his own hand, and not that of a later biographer, that we can be reasonably certain of the dates which matter,

Not so certain are the details of our next saint. An ancient 'life' of St Carantoc, written in Latin is held in the British Museum and it tells of a saint who could trace his genealogy back to the Virgin Mary, and who left his native Cardiganshire in Wales to travel to Ireland in order to help Patrick with his mission.

The 'life' tells us that the two men met together in unity and that they agreed to work in two different regions of Ireland, meeting up once a year. We are also told that in Ireland, Carantoc made a name for himself by his mighty works. Known sometimes as Cernach or Cernacus, he built churches and towns and wherever he was, "he healed thousands of men filled with various pains – blind, lame, lunatic and such like. He was a marvellous spiritual and supreme abbot, a long suffering teacher of fidelity, announcing righteousness to all the righteous, a herald of the heavenly kingdom."

In the Leon Breviary in Brittany, Carantoc is sometimes known as Caradoc. The lessons tell the story of Carantoc, in Ireland, asking a local land owner for permission to fell a large tree so that he could begin the building of a monastery. The owner challenged him to call upon his God to fell the tree, saying, "Call upon thy God, and if it fall it is thine." Carantoc answered "Nothing is impossible to God." When he had finished his prayer, the tree fell.

In the same Breviary there is an important story which gives credence to Carantoc's involvement in Cornwall and Brittany. This story is also found in a 17th century work by Albert Le Grand who compiled a work on the saints of Brittany. The manuscript Albert Le Grand uses was obtained as part of a collection of manuscripts found in the Cathedral Church of Leon. The story concerns another saint called, in Brittany, Tenenan or Tinidor, who was known in Cornwall as Enoder, pronounced locally as Ineder.

Tenenan/ Enoder was the son of an Irish prince and a pupil of Carantoc. After completing his studies, his parents sent him to the king's court in London where the only daughter of the Count of Arundel fell in love with him. Tenenan, who had a longing to become a monk, was horrified when wedding plans were put in place and he prayed, long and hard, that God would make him so ugly that no-one would ever want to marry him. His prayer was heard and he contracted leprosy. The wedding was called off and Tenenan returned happily to Ireland.

On arrival in Ireland he went to see Carantoc. After feeding the boy, Carantoc prepared a bath for him and the moment Carantoc touched Tenenan's skin to wash him, the leprosy left him and he was clean once more. Tenenan was hesitant to rejoice saying that now he was free of the leprosy he was in danger of becoming proud because of his good looks. Carantoc replied "You shall be fairer but now your skin will not stink!"

We know that Carantoc returned to Cardiganshire and that he visited Somerset and it would appear that,accompanied by some of his young students, including Tenenan, he travelled on to Cornwall, landing at the mouth of the Gannel. We don't know if Carantoc left his work in Ireland before or after the death of Patrick but, we believe that he was getting old himself and, if we put his arrival in Cornwall as being between AD450 and AD 470 we wouldn't be too far out.

It would appear that Carantoc and his disciples followed the same plan as other pilgrim saints. They first built and established their 'mother' church and then the disciples were sent, one by one to establish their own.

We are not sure how many young people accompanied Carantoc, possibly seven. Nicholas Roscarrock, who wrote in the 16th century, tells us that every year people, from seven different churches round about, gathered at the church at Crantock, bringing with them relics which were honoured on seven different altars.

In order to have an idea as to who these saints were, it is necessary to follow their journey, and see if the names of the church dedications close to Kerentec in Brittany match those in Cornwall close to Crantock. The church of St Enoder is the most obvious one. It is within 5 miles of Crantock in Cornwall and there are three church dedications to Tenenan within 3 miles of Kerentec and a further 8 within a wider 20 miles. Other dedications found in both areas are to St Columb, St Colan, St Newlyn (in Brittany Nol-uen) and St Cubert. In the parish of St Enoder there was once a chapel beside a spring in Indian Queens and the remains of a very early convent in Fraddon. Their dedications are not remembered.

The party didn't travel far in Brittany. They stayed within the Diocese of St Pol de Leon and we know that Tenenan/Enoder found a 'desert' place for himself at a place now called Lan Tinidor near the tidal river of Ylorna. Tenenan eventually became Bishop of Leon and, when he was consecrated and a statue of him was being made, he arranged instead for it to be of St Carantoc, his beloved teacher, with himself as a small child at Carantoc's feet.

Patrick and Carantoc were both Romano British Celts. Patrick's loyalties lay with Rome while Carantoc came from the refugee population that had settled in the Welsh valleys. They had very different ideas about theology and liturgy, but it seems that each recognised in the other, a person chosen and loved by God: a person worthy of great respect. Wisely, they decided to meet up only once a year.

CHAPTER EIGHT

Teachers and students in Wales

Two of the best known of the teachers in Wales in the early days of the new movement, which we have come to know as the Celtic Christian Church, were Dubricius (AD 465-550) and Illtyd (AD 480-540).

It is necessary to understand that the west and north of England were not empty wastelands. The west, in particular, was populated by many important Romano British families and a large number of retired military officers and men. And when Vortigern moved the capital to Gloucester, the area became quite crowded with important families. They were sophisticated and wealthy, and were settled, mostly around the Severn estuary, close to the port and the old Roman barracks. There were, indeed, large tracts of unoccupied land which had been cleared by the Cornovii in the area we now call Powys, and it is in the valleys of Powys where the fleeing Britons found sanctuary. The land to the north and north east of Britain, in Cumbria and Northumberland, also attracted the refugees as it was open and sparcely peopled.

In the west, the established church, known to the Romanised families, continued to operate, but, although some clung steadfastly to the Roman ways, it was not long before the lack of contact with Rome and the influence of the new teaching began to take a hold. Dubricius and Illtyd were two of the most important teachers to herald the change.

According to his 'life', Dubricius, born in AD 465, was the illegitimate son of Efrddyl, the daughter of King Peibo Clafrog of Ergyng. When the king discovered his daughter was pregnant, he had her thrown into the River Wye. Efrddyl survived and clambered ashore, close to Madley, in Herefordshire, where Dubricius was born.

Dubricius was an extremely intelligent child and, as a scholar, he excelled in his studies of the Old and New Testaments.

He founded monasteries at both Hentland and Moccas, where his pupils included both Samson and Teilo, and he was known, in the area, for his healing miracles and his kindly demeanour. He may have travelled to Somerset at some time as there is a dedication to him at Porlock, on the Exmoor coast.

He was made Bishop of Ergyng (Caerleon and Llandoff) but resigned the position in AD 545 in favour of David and retired to his 'desert' place on Bardsley Island, where he died.
Legend says that he was the Bishop to crown Arthur.

Illtyd, born in AD 480, was often known as Illtyd Farehog, or Illtyd the Knight. According to his 'life' he was, as a young man, a knight in Arthur's army. As a child he had been brought up by his parents and teachers to go into the Church, but, it seems that the young Illtyd was captivated instead by the excitement of being part of Arthur's army. It was the red martyrdom he sought. After serving for several years in the army, the religious life tugged again at his heart, and he, then, left the army and became a disciple of Bishop Germanus. Eventually he established his own school of Divinity at Cor Tewdws in Llantwit Major, in Glamorgan. As an abbot /teacher his fame spread throughout the western world. It is calculated that his pupils numbered in their thousands and included Paul Aurelian, David, and the historian Gildas.
The wealthy families sent their children to teachers such as these. They usually went to the teachers when they were 5 years old, and left in their late teens. The schools were run on monastic lines, similar to the monasteries first set up by Martin and, as these youngsters went through the system and out into the world, it was the monasteries which grew in importance and which developed a greater influence among the people, rather than the more traditional and more exclusive church system of the past.
Both Dubricius and Illtyd were gentle, moderate teachers who discouraged extremism of every kind. They preferred to inspire rather than correct, and their pupils loved them for it.
In true Celtic style, when Illtyd retired, he spent his last years as a hermit and died in his 'desert' place at Llaniltud, in the Vale of Glamorgan. The year was AD 540.

A contempory of Dubricius and Illtyd was the monk Ailbe. Ailbe's father fled from King Cronan of Ireland, before Ailbe was born. The king then ordered the servants to put the new born child to death. Unable to kill a small baby, the servants put the child on a flat rock next to a road, hoping that a passer by would take him home. The story continues with the baby being cared for and nursed by a she-wolf, before, eventually, being found and fostered by British parents who returned with him to Wales and brought him up. Long afterwards, when Ailbe was a bishop, an old she-wolf was being hunted and ran to Ailbe for safety. She laid her head on his breast and Ailbe protected her and her cubs, and continued to feed them daily at his Bishop's Hall. We know very little about him except that his earliest 'life' tells us that he travelled to Rome as a young monk and he was consecrated bishop by Pope Hilary. We know, too, that his ministry was in Wales and that he became Bishop at Menevia (St David's). The 'life' of David tells us that Ailbe was there at David's birth.

The monastery schools in Wales were set up, originally, for boys alone, but, as time went on, some of them became co-educational. David's mother, Nonna, was a student at the monastery school of Ty Gwyn. She was from a noble family which had settled close by. While she was at the school, she fell in love with a visiting student named Sant. Sant did not stay long and, when he moved away, Nonna realised that she was pregnant. Somehow she managed to keep it a secret until the time came for her to give birth. She slipped away from the monastery and climbed the hill to a mountain hut which was near the standing stones beyond Bryn Y Garn. Here she gave birth to a still born baby boy.

In utter distress, she had no idea what to do and was relieved when the kindly monk Ailbe suddenly appeared, took the baby from her and plunged it quickly in an icy, cold pool of water. The baby gasped and then breathed.

Because of the disgrace of having an illegitimate child, Nonna could not return to the monastery or to her family. Instead, Ailbe agreed to foster the baby and bring him up in a monastery, while Nonna decided to go as far away as possible. The baby was given the name of David.

On her own, travelling would have been dangerous , but Nonna made it as far as Cornwall.

In Cornwall, it is possible that Nonna went first to Crida by the River Fal. Both from noble families there was likely to be a connection and the older woman was wise and experienced and would have been a good counsellor for a frightened, young woman. Close to Crida's nunnery was once a small chapel dedicated to St Nonna. Today, in the village of Grampound, there is a Victorian mission church on the site, which still bears her name.

Her main church is found at Altarnun in the middle of Bodmin Moor. The adjacent parish is Davidstow and it is thought that, later, David visited his mother and stayed long enough to establish a church which later became dedicated to him. His father, Sant, is remembered at Sancreed which used to be called Eglos-Sant, and the village of St. Breoke was originally called Lansant.

Brought up in a monastic setting, David never experienced the comforts of home He was raised in the strict tradition of the more ascetic of the monks who were known as meloires meaning 'better'. These monks particularly infuriated the historian Gildas who accused them of thinking themselves better than everyone else. Their goal was to imitate the asceticism of Antony of Egypt and in doing so they went to absolute extremes. They spent all day-light hours in vigorous labour and their evenings were spent in studying. They scorned the use of employed labourers and draught animals and insisted on doing everything themselves, including the ploughing and digging. Their food was bread, cabbage and water and they wore the simplest of clothing. Nothing they used or wore belonged to them personally but to the whole group. Theirs was a rule which required little talking and absolute obedience. Dubricius and Illtyd, who were far more relaxed, thought that the pride these monks felt in being so strict was a danger to their souls. They themselves were noblemen who taught classical learning and the scriptures and who were gentle with their students. They knew that young men could be inclined to be hard on themselves and felt that kind words and understanding was an effective way of getting them to be aware of the dangers.

When David had finished his studies, he travelled thoughout Wales preaching the Gospel and founding new communities. His last community was in Mynyw, where he built an abbey and where he eventually died.

With his fellow monks he was often stern and unyielding but with the people who came to him he was kind and caring.

Gildas, the historian was a pupil of Illtyd and in his book, 'The Ruin of Britain,' he holds no punches. David and the 'meloires' might be at one end of the spectrum but at the other extreme were those who called themselves Christians and yet behaved outrageously and selfishly and made the lives of those dependent on them, miserable. In his book, he calls out Constantine of Cornwall, as we have mentioned before, and also Aurelius Conanus of Gloucester and Cuneglasse of Ross in Gwynedd, all warlords, and warns them that the manner in which they treated their subjects would be exactly the way they, themselves, would be treated in Hell.

With the death of Arthur all semblance of a coherent government in western Britain gradually came to an end and this heralded the time of the local kings or warlords. The time of the great bishops of the ancient dioceses also began to come to an end. Every king or warlord wanted a bishop of his own.

In AD 594 Augustine (of Canterbury) landed in Kent to bring the Gospel to the pagan Angles and Saxons. Sent by Pope Gregory and by going immediately to the Saxon royalty he was received well and began to make converts. Anxious to link up

with the Celtic Church in the west, he sent an invitation to the Celtic bishops asking them to join him in a conference at an unrecorded meeting place, somewhere in Gloucestershire or Wiltshire. Remembering what had happened at the Hengist and Vortigern summit, the bishops were not inclined to accept. But they agreed to take the advice of the Church elders who persuaded them to make the journey on one condition. If, when they arrived at the conference, they were treated with dignity, they should remain and talk, but if they were treated with disdain, they were not to stay.
Seven Celtic bishop's made the journey on foot, and when they arrived at the conference they were tired and their robes were muddy and wet. Augustine was sitting on a high chair. His bishop's robes were immaculate and he was surrounded by his priests and deacons. The Celtic bishops stood at the door and waited to be called forward but Augustine was busy talking and ignored them. According to the historian Bede, the bishops looked at each other in silence and then turned and walked all the way home again. Augustine lost his one opportunity to link with the breakaway Celtic British Church.

The early 6th century became a time of change and confusion, all in the name of Christianity. Monasteries, following the pattern of Marmoutier, were being established in the estates of the Christian, noble landowners. The abbots, who were appointed to run them, became important and powerful and often challenged the older established bishops by arranging for the consecration of one of their own monks to be a bishop under obedience to the abbot. These bishops had no administrative duties, as these were undertaken by the abbot. Instead, the monastic bishops could preach, baptise and ordain priests and often were given licence to leave the monasteries to become travelling evangelists, provided they returned, when needed. In addition the bishops, who were appointed by the various kings, were often not consecrated properly and many did not really want to be bishops at all. And in all of this disorganisation, hundreds of the young, enthusiastic students were ready to leave their schools to begin their martyrdoms.
In Wales some semblance of order was restored, as the most important abbots continued to serve as bishops in the original major dioceses, but in the south west and Brittany where Christianity was new, order was totally in the hands of the kings and warlords, And as we have seen from the story of Conomorus and his family, this could be either a blessing or a curse.
It is no wonder that the young people wanted, more than ever, to go and find their

own 'deser't place. Somewhere where they could be far away from the political chaos and be at one with the sea and the sky, or at peace in a forest glade. Somewhere where they could stand alone in the presence of Christ. All around the coasts of Devon and Cornwall, of Wales, Ireland, Scotland and northern England, every cave or forest glade was occupied. These young saints left their mark on the very edge of the world. They went as far as they could, to be alone.

CHAPTER NINE

Samson, the children of Brychan, and Petroc

By following the life of the young monk Samson, we can glimpse a little of the situation in the early 6th century. Samson came from a wealthy, land owning family and attended the schools of both Dubricius and Illtyd. Illtyd, with his moderate outlook, is recorded as gently chiding Samson for his tendency to be too hard on himself. In this he must have been quite successful because, later in life, Samson had cause to look upon David's extremes with a certain amount of horror.

As a child Samson was considered a genius. He found learning easy and he outpaced his fellow students very quickly. In his early 20s, he was informed that his father was dying and returned home. His father recovered and both parents, along with his younger brothers, became new and committed Christians. They took monastic vows and gave most of their property to the poor.

At the death of the abbot of the monastery on Caldey island, Samson was persuaded to take his place. As an abbot, Samson was strict with the monks, but not excessively so. Still, they were relieved when he left, and he was relieved to be free. He found an abandoned castle by the Severn, but, after an uncomfortable time, he moved into a cave. He enjoyed the solitude, but a cold and wet cave in Wales could not compare with Antony's cave in the hot deserts of Egypt. A synod decided that he was needed in the diocese and he allowed himself to be consecrated bishop. But, very soon afterwards he had a vision and, w,hile he was still in his late 30s, he decided to find his own 'desert place', and, saying farewell to his family, he set off by sea to Cornwall.

In Cornwall he went straight to the monastery founded by Docco at St Kew, and asked if he could stay for a while. Abbot Iuniavis was apologetic but had obviously heard of Samson's fervour and was anxious not to allow his himself and his monks to be embarrassed by this fine young saint. According to Samson's 'life,' written by his cousin Enoch, 30 years after Samson's death, Iuniavis says

"beloved father, it is better for the servant of God to continue his journey..... your request to stay with us is inconvenient, for you are 'melior', better than us; you might condemn us and we might properly feel condemned by your superior merit; for I must make it clear to you that we have somewhat relaxed our original rules... You had better go on... to Europe."

Duly shocked by this, Samson, unloaded his books and his religious paraphernalia frm the boat, put them in a wagon and trekked off on foot across Cornwall, along what has since been called the 'Saint's Way', from Padstow to Fowey. This route took him across Bodmin Moor where he came across a group of locals, seemingly worshipping around a standing stone. (This seems to confirm the thought that civilisation at this time in Cornwall was found mostly around the rivers and coasts, and that the inland areas were still inhabited by a pagan population.) Samson strode over to the group and imperiously stopped the celebration and carved a cross on the stone, preached to them and insisted that they should honour the cross. He warned them that he would pass that way again and he expected find them still faithful to Christ.

Samson went on to Castle Dore where he stayed for a while before getting a boat to Brittany. In Brittany, however, he was not allowed to be a hermit for long and he became bishop in the kingdom of Jonas of Dumnonie, with his see at Dol, and as, thanks to his consecration near the Severn, he was the only bishop in the area who had been canonically consecrated, he was regarded with great respect

In Brittany, Samsom established many monasteries and churches and, eventually, died around AD 560. In all ,we know of 26 churches and chapels in the north and east of Brittany which bear his name. He is spoken of with reverence in Wales, Cornwall and Brittany. His passionate nature and his zeal for Christ mark him out as an outstanding example of a Celtic Christian saint.

A large number of young saints are recorded as having come from mid and south Wales, and many of them appear to have come from the region of Brecon. They are often referred to as the Children of Brychan. King Brychan is supposed to have had 24 children by his wife, Gladwys, who travelled as missionaries to Cornwall. The story borders on the fanciful and the lists of these children's names vary considerably and, apart from Nectan, none of the names recorded in Wales match with any of those recorded in Cornwall. There is no question that hundreds of young people from Wales travelled to Cornwall and many of them went on to Brittany. It is also quite likely that many travelled together. Were these young people all from the same family, or perhaps from the same monastic school? Canon Doble makes yet another suggestion and says that, "it is a well known fact that the tribe of the Cornovii, who gave their name to Cornwall, moved from central Wales to the end of the Dumnonian peninsula about the 4th or 5th century. May not the fact that so many places in east Cornwall are called after the 'children of Brychan,' have some connection with the great migration which gave Cornwall its name?"

It is not possible to tell the story of all the young Welsh saints, but there is one more which is really very important, and that is of Petroc.
Canon Doble tells us that St. Petroc probably came from south-east Wales and was from the royal house of Gwent. In his life, written within a 100 years of his death by someone from his monastery in Bodmin, we read that he was the first born son of the king and was expected to succeed him. At his father's death, however, Petroc refused the crown in order to give himself to Christ, and his brother took the crown instead. Petroc chose to go to Ireland to study because he believed that the teachers were better in Ireland and, after his studies, he set sail for Cornwall and settled in Padstow where he established a school. He attracted so many students and disciples that it was necessary to build more accommodation and this he did, at nearby Little Petherick.
Petroc found that he was under such pressure from eager students that he hardly had time to pray and he decided to take some time out and visit Rome and Jerusalem. How long he was away we are not told, but his schools and his pupils were still there when he returned. Again, he set to, and began once again to teach. The 'life' includes stories of him rising at cockcrow and standing up to his neck in the icy cold water of the sea until sunrise, praying and reciting the Psalms. This was his quiet time, before the daily task of dealing with students' questions began again. I wonder if teachers today might consider this discipline as a way of preparing themselves for a day at school!
Pupils came to him from miles away and his fame spread throughout the world of the Celtic diaspora and, yet again, Petroc became exhausted. This time he walked inland to a huge forested area where Goran, an old friend from Wales, was living in solitude. When Petroc found him, he was overcome with the beauty and serenity of the forest glade and the little hermitage beside a spring. After a night of wonderful sleep, Petroc asked his old friend if he could stay, and Goran said that during the night he had had a dream and he knew that Petroc was going to ask this question, so he had had time to think. He said he would be pleased if Petroc would make this place his home, but he knew that it would not be long before Petroc's students found their master and this quiet place would be quiet no longer, so he had already packed his bag and would go and find another 'desert' place for himself.
He went a day's journey and settled close to the south coast, near to the hermitage of a childhood friend called Yestin (Just), a mile beyond Mevagissey.
He was right about Petroc's students. They found him, and the forest became forest no longer. He built an even larger monastery school there, with a chapel next to the

spring. And the town which formed around it was called Dinuurin (Goran's town), now known as Bodmin. Goran's spring can still be found, close to the main door of Bodmin's parish church.
When Petroc felt that he was close to death he walked back to Padstow, where he died, and his body was buried in the churchyard. But, when the priory at Bodmin was completed, Petroc's bones were removed to the new church and his head, and some of the bones, were kept in an ivory casket which was approximately 18 inches long and ornately carved, and kept in a shrine near the altar. Some time later it was hidden in the small room above the south door and was not discovered until the 18th century. The box no longer holds the bones of Petroc and has been stolen, and returned, on two separate occasions, once by monks from St Meen(Mewan) in Brittany and, lately, by thieves at the end of the 20th Century. It is now safely cared for by the parish of Bodmin.

Petroc was an obsessive, but dedicated, teacher who worked himself to death, so determined was he to put the interests of his students first. His 'life' does not tell us of his work in Devon but there are even more dedications to him there, than there are in Cornwall. There is a legend that tells us that when the canons of Bodmin had taken the casket to the Court of Henry Ist and were returning, they stopped for the night on Dartmoor. During the night their horses managed to get loose and damaged a field of corn. A crowd of angry peasants assembled and began to threaten the party from Bodmin. The canons ordered the servants to pack up their belongings and to get on the way as quickly as possible. The 12 men guarding the casket carried it behind the main party and the hostile peasants followed them. Suddenly a pillar of fire issued from the casket, rising into the heavens, and the peasants scattered, in fear of their lives. As I have said before, it is not wise to mess with teachers!

CHAPTER TEN

Winwaloe, St Mawes, St Mewan and St Austoll

Our next story invoves a saint, who was the son of a Dumnonian (Devon and Cornwall) leader, who had decided to leave Britain with his family and find new lands for himself in Brittany. Compared to the land in Dumnonia, which was rocky and sparce, the land in Brittany was fertile and vast. Many estates had been abandoned by Roman families who had returned to Rome, and those who reached the deserted lands first had a chance of becoming rich. A pestilence occurred in Dumnonia and Fracan decided to take the chance. Taking his pregnant wife and his three children, he left Britain and landed at Brahec and, immediately, started looking for abandoned land. It didn't take long and he found an estate, surrounded by woods and bordered by a stream. He took possession of it and made it his home. A baby boy was born soon after and he was named, Winwaloe in the British tongue, Guenole in Breton, also frequently known as Wennec or Wednac. In Britain he is remembered at Gunwaloe, Landewednack, Towednack and Tremaine, and in Britanny there are several dedications but, by far the most important, is the great monastery of Landevennec, close to Quimper. His 'life' was written by the monk Wrdisten, from Landevennec, about 200 years after Winwaloe's death.

When Winwaloe was 5 years old, his parents took him to a teacher called Budoc. Under Budoc's guidance, the child flourished and it wasn't long before he had made rapid advances in his studies.

Even as a child he performed healing miracles, healing a fellow student's broken leg, curing his sister of blindness, curing another student who was bitten by a snake and healing a rider thrown from a horse.

Winwaloe had an ambition to go to Ireland to help the great saint Patrick, but when he was finally old enough to leave Budoc, he had a dream in which Patrick, himself, appeared to him and told him to stay and do the Lord's work in Brittany. The next day he told Budoc of the dream and Budoc gave him 11 of the other students and sent them all off to begin their mission. The little group walked towards the west and finally reached the coast at the estuary of the River Aulne. Ahead of them, a little way off shore, was the small island of Tibidy. Winwaloe encouraged them to wade through the waters and to reach the island, and decided that it would make an ideal place to settle and make his monastery. It wasn't. It was far too small for such a large group. It was exposed to the wind and weather and the soil was thin and rocky. Unwilling

to give up, they stayed there for three miserable years but finally Winwaloe gave way to his disciples' pleas and they went ashore on the banks of the estuary and found a sheltered, sunny spot and began to build their monastery all over again. Compared to the wind blasted island, this new land was heaven. And so it proved to be. They stayed in the same spot and grew old together and nobody died. Again, the disciples went to their master and begged him to build a new monastery a stone's throw away from the first, because they believed that, as they were already in heaven, they would never die, and their bodies were getting old and there was no longer a joy in living. The new monastery was built and the monks moved, and one by one, the disciples thankfully died. When Winwaloe knew that he too would die, he offered Mass, and when he had received the bread and wine, he stood before the altar, supported by two monks, and yielded up his spirit.
Winwaloe lived his entire adult life in his monastery. We don't know if he ever travelled to Ireland as he had wished to do as a child. He may have done, or perhaps some of his young monks made the trip. On Cornwall's southern-most tip is the little harbour of Lanewednack and around the corner on a sandy beach facing west is the church of Winwaloe. Close to the north coast is the church and village of Towednack. All these places are ideally situated for the coming and going of boats from Brittany to Ireland. There are also churches dedicated to Winwaloe in Tremaine and Portlemouth in Devon.
Winwaloe's body was buried first under the old church but later it was transferred to the new church until in the 10th century when the Norseman invaders plundered the lands of nothern France. Tthe monks of Landevennec fled and took Winwaloe's bones, his bell and his vestments to the monastery of Saint Sauve, near Montreuil, for safe keeping. The body of Samson went to Orleans, while the body of St Maudez was taken to Bourges.

The Abbey at Landevennec was very much a Celtic foundation. It retained the pattern of individual cells or huts around a central church. The monks wore St Martin's tonsure and each monk strove to live frugally. Winwaloe, himself, was known to be a strict abbot who preferred his monks to live in silence. When Louis the Pious met the abbot of the time in AD 818, he was taken aback to see that he was still using St Martin's tonsure and insisted that the abbey should cease to be such an extreme order, and that it should become a Benedictine foundation instead. As it still is today. The monks at Landevennec, today, are a silent order but they encourage visitors to join them in their prayers. It is a place of great peace and the Guest House, called

La Penite, is built on the site of the original monastery and, like Winwaloe's elderly monks, it is still possible to feel that the stairway to heaven reaches to the ground in this very spot. As a community the monks are particularly interested in ecumenical relationships and welcome visitors to make use of the space they are offered, to make friends across the many different divides. There is a particular link with the churches in Cornwall, made in 1987 by Abbot Jean de la Croix and Bishop Peter Mumford of Truro, and frequent visits are made between the two Celtic regions.

Our next saint is known as Maudez in Brittany and St Mawes in Cornwall. He has had two 'lives' written about him but neither tells us very much. The first 'life' was written 600 years after his death, and the second was written in the 14th century.
We are told that Maudetus was the tenth child of King Ercleus and Queen Gentusa of Ireland and that Maudez was given, at the age of seven, to the service of God, as a tithe. The names of his family, however, are British, and not Irish, so it is thought that the biographer should have made Wales his birthplace, and not Ireland. Nothing more is said about his childhood and the next we hear, is of him travelling to Brittany with a large number of disciples. Finding an island off the north coast he banished all snakes from the island and the group built their huts and a small church and made it their first foundation. Maudez worked many miracles of healing, especially healing people of intestinal worms and headaches. He was considered to be an exceptional teacher. There is a special rock on his island on which he was supposed to have sat, while he was teaching. There are three small islands in the bay of Saint Brieuc, one named Ile Modez, (Mawes), another named Ile Lavret, the island of the teacher Budoc , and one named Ile Brehat whose chapel is dedicated to Samson. All three islands mark the landing places of three important teachers. The ruins of the first small foundations they built can be seen on the islands and it is from these rocky, isolated places that the teachers sent their disciples out to found their own churches. Maudez spent the rest of his life on the island, teaching and preaching and healing all who came to him. He eventually died on his island and the cult of St Maudez sprang into existence and spread all over France. He is now the patron of about 60 churches and chapels. Wherever there is a chapel or statue of St Maudez, a pinch of earth is scraped up and mixed with water and drunk by the sick, particularly by those suffering from worms.
As in Brittany, the dedication to St Mawes in Cornwall is close to that of St Budoc. St Mawes is on the east bank of the estuary of the River Fal while, almost directly opposite, on the west side, lies the parish of St Budoc.

Another two saints who are intimately connected with Brittany are Austol and Mewan(Me'en or Mevennus). It is believed that Mewan was a cousin of Samson, and that, with Petroc, Austol, Melorius, Touinian (Towan), Sulian and several others, they all travelled with Samson. They came from the same area in Gwent and it looks as though they all stayed for a few years in Cornwall ,before going on to Brittany. Each, it would appear, set up their foundations in the southern area of Cornwall, within walking distance of each other. Austol chose to make his foundation into a hermitage, next to a spring in the middle of a forest. On a hill close by, the more adventurous Mewan made his foundation. As Mewan's full name was Conaidus Mevennus, it is possible that he was also the Conan who set up the original foundation at Roche, the dedication of which was changed later, to Gomondus.

Building a Celtic foundation would not have taken long. Ever since the time of Martin at Marmoutier the pattern of the little monasteries remained the same: a circle of wooden or stone huts around a small church, and close to a spring of pure water. The church, most likely, had stone walls and a thatched or turfed roof with an earthen floor. To have an idea of how one looked it would be advisable to travel to Madron in the far west of Cornwall and see for yourself the remains of the 7th century baptistry. (grid reference) (photo)

The Celtic monasteries all began in this way and the archaelogical remains of hundreds of them are now impossible to find. Where the huts were built of stone on the barren islands or cliff tops, some evidence often remains but, on the whole, the wet weather of the maritime fringes of Europe has obliterated all trace. The best clues we have in all of this are the place names. The names hold the memories of the people.

After a few years the party moved on to Brittany and we have a 'life' of Mewan to tell us more of the story.

When they landed in Brittany, the group stayed with Samson on the island of Levrat near Dol, and together built his little monastery, with enough huts for visitors. When they came to building the church, Samson sent Mewan as his spokes- person to ask the nearby landowner, Count Gueric, for assistance. On his way Mewan met a lonely, very elderly man, who was walking along the riverside. The man's name was Cadvon. He invited Mewan to stay the night and the two men became good friends. Mewan continued his journey to Gueric, who agreed to help Samson with his building project, and Mewan called in on his new friend on the return journey. Cadvon had no children, but had a large house and vast lands and he became like a father to Mewan, bequeathing him all his lands and property. On this land Mewan, eventually,

built his own monastic foundation and school.
It would seem that Austol remained with Mewan when the others left to seek a place for their own foundations. Perhaps he built a hermitage for himself in the vast grounds. Here the two men lived for the rest of their lives, passing their days in prayer and vigil, offering themselves as a living sacrifice unto the Lord. Mewan's fame spread and pupils came from all over France, and his monks practised a rigid self denial. He received countless gifts of land and money and arranged for the building of many more monasteries.
In his old age, he began to feel frail and his old friend, Austol, was constantly by his side, supporting and helping him, and, when Mewan died, Austol was inconsolable. Mewan's body was laid in a tomb and seven days later, Austol himself died. Knowing how close the two friends had been, the monks decided to bury Austol beside Mewan, in the same tomb. When they opened Mewan's tomb, they discovered that Mewan's body, which they had laid in the middle, had moved to one side, leaving space for Austol's body to lie beside it.

Today the church of St Austell, which was built over Austol's hermitage, is in the middle of a large town, which is also named for him. The church of St Mewan, over Mewan's first foundation, is on the hill to the south of the town close to a school and a small hamlet.

CHAPTER ELEVEN

The Church in Ireland and some important Irish saints

During the 6th Century AD Pope Gregory sent Bishop Augustine to Kent to take Christianity to the Angles and Saxons and to bring the Celtic Church in the west back in to the fold of the Catholic Church. Augustine managed to establish a foothold for Christ in Canterbury and his mission to the invaders was successful but he was unable to make friends with the Celtic Church who regarded him with great suspicion. When he died in AD 604 the Celtic Curch was still stubbornly independent. The Church which was established by Patrick in Ireland had, however, managed to retain its links with Rome and keep its succession of consecrated bishops, with their sees, in acceptable order. Even though the theology of the Irish church was largely Celtic, there was pride in the fact that they were part of the Holy Catholic church. Substantial monasteries and schools were established and, as people began to settle to farming instead of fighting, these schools began to attract young people from northern Britain and from all over Europe.

From a very early time the schools in Ireland were co-educational and, when the students completed their studies, several of the girls took vows and formed religious establishments, and many went with the young men on their missionary journeys.

Whereas the teachers in Wales, Cornwall and Brittany were very firmly influenced by Martin, and had followed his manner of teaching, in buildings which were simple and built on land which was often poor, Patrick, in the traditional manner, insisted that when the rich gave land for monasteries, it should be the best land possible. As a result, the monasteries in Ireland flourished and grew in size. They may have started as small, insignificant huts around a church but they soon grew to be large, imposing stone buildings, attracting many students.

The most famous of the Irish women saints is Brigid. She was a child when Patrick died in AD 461. Her mother was slave girl who had been made pregnant by her master, and his wife had insisted that the slave girl should be sold. The pregnant girl was sold to a Druid priest, but, somehow, managed to keep her faith and pass it on to her daughter, and Brigid grew up to be both modest and gentle.

When she was 18, her step father tried to arrange a marriage for her but she refused and ran away, deciding instead to enter one of the new nunneries. This was the choice of many young women of the time and Brigid had to wait in line for her turn to be interviewed by the bishop, in order to see if she would be accepted. Legend tells us that, as she waited, the bishop looked up and saw a pillar of light surrounding her, and he called her forward, ahead of the others in the queue. When she came to him he gave her his blessing, but not the one for a new postulant but the blessing for a bishop. When he was questioned about this he replied, "I have no power. The dignity has already been given to her by God."

Brigid's fame spread far and wide, and many wealthy nobles donated land and riches for her to build a monastery and school. Her foundation at Kildare in Leinster, became known as 'the city of the poor' because of her hospitality. There she lit a fire which she and her nuns tended, keeping it alight as a symbol of faith. The nuns of her foundation continued to keep it alight for a full 1000 years after her death. She died in AD 525 and, within a century, of her death she was made a national saint, second only to Patrick.

It has to be noted here, that, as Ireland had remained under the control of the Roman church and, as the necessary regulations were met, the Pope would have no reservations about sanctifying Brigid. But it was an entirely different matter with the British Church. They were going it alone and had very few links with the Roman Church at all. The hundreds of teachers and their young students who were revered locally by everyone for their holiness, and for their wonderful miracles, were never officially made saints. When the British churches of the west eventually came under the wing of the Roman Church once more, the monks at the individual British monasteries, anxious that their founder should be recognised as truly saintly, set about writing their saint's 'life.' This explains why the 'lives' often appear to be so full of the stories of rather fanciful miracles. The Roman Church required three proven miracles to be directly connected to the saint, before they would consider veneration. Unfortunately, sending a dragon into exile didn't cut the mustard!

Another Irish holy woman was Beriana, of whom we heard earlier when she healed Erbin. Unfortunately we don't know much more about her life. She may have travelled to Cornwall with a large number of other Irish saints who landed in the Hayle estuary. We do know that she lived first beside a spring at a hamlet known as Alsia, which is a mile to the north-east of St Buryan, and that she attracted many pilgrims because of her remarkable healing powers. She was given land and money from grateful families and founded a monastery, built in the traditional Celtic manner with small huts around a church and enclosed by a wall or fence. If you travel to St. Buryan in

Cornwall, you can see that the oval shaped outer wall of her monastic enclosure is still there in the middle of the village. The earth inside the enclosure has risen to the top of the wall because of the continual burials over the years. The large church that stands over the original church was built with money given by King Athelstan in AD 930, up until which time the monastic settlement was still being run on Celtic lines. For all her good works and her popularity, Beriana was never recognised by the Roman C,hurch as a saint. Had she stayed in Ireland the outcome might have been very different. As it was, her church became a shrine and was visited by loyal Cornish families for many years.

The group of Irish saints which landed at Hayle, was led by Gwinnear. We don't know exactly how many young people travelled together but it is believed that a large number of churches were established in the west of Cornwall by Irish saints, all at round about the same time. These are St Erc, St Phillack, St Gwithian, St Germoe, St Anta, St Breage, St Euny, St Fingar and St. Crowan. The legend tells us that St Ia (Ives) missed the boat and travelled over from Ireland on a leaf (coracle?), landing a little further to the west of the others. This was a lucky accident, as the arrival of so many young people on the Hayle sands, alerted the authorities, who thought this was an aggressive Irish invasion, and charged down on to the beach to prevent them from landing. Some were injured or killed before it was realised that they had come in peace. According to the 'life' of Gwinnear, his head was chopped off and, not wanting to die on the beach, he picked it up and walked a mile inland until he found a fresh spring, and,washing his head carefully, he laid it gently down on the grass, and then he lay down and died. Even for that miracle he was not officially sainted.

We have very few details of the travelling Irish missionaries, and the same can be said about Cornwall's patron saint, St Piran. We are not even sure who he was. There are two 'lives' of Piran to choose from. One tells us that he annoyed an Irish chieftan and was put in a barrel which was dropped off a cliff and fell into the sea. Eventually the tides washed him up on the sands of north Cornwall. The second 'life' was written by a monk, from the diocese of Exeter, who retells the life of a famous monk from Ireland called Ciaran and replaces his name with that of Piran, making us believe that they are one and the same, which they may well be. There is a third possibility. There is an old chapel in Cardiff dedicated to St. Peran, making him Welsh rather than Irish. Whoever he was, he built an oratory on the shore at Perranporth, which eventually became covered by sand and had to be built further inland. Several

churches in Cornwall are dedicated to St.Piran and they are placed strategically along routes leading from the north to the south coasts, indicating that either Piran, or his disciples, regularly crossed Cornwall, crossing and recrossing from Ireland or Wales and on to Brittany. There is a statue of St.Piran in the little church at Trezelide near Pol de Leon and yet another roadside statue nearby, of St Piran at prayer.
In Cornwall, St Piran has been adopted as the patron saint of tinners and the Cornish flag is often called St Piran's flag. It is a white cross against a black background and is thought to represent a white hot seam of tin in the black granite which was seen when Piran made a fire on the rocks of the beach, in order to make a brew. As mentioned before, the white cross on the flags of Devon and Cornwall, actually commemorate the young British saints of the white martyrdom who brought the Christian faith to the land, just as the red cross on the banners of Arthur's young soldiers indicated their red martyrdom and their willingness to die to protect their faith.
On the 5th of March each year, St.Piran's feast day is commemorated on the dunes at Perranporth. His stories are re-enacted and his oratories are visited and the day ends at the cross of St. Piran which stands in front of the ruins of the medieval church. Its often a cold and windy day but, as St Piran is also known for his love of the hard stuff, his followers know exactly how they should keep warm!

Another wandering Irishman whom we should mention, is Brendan. Instead of travelling south, he chose, instead, to travel to the far north-west. In his 'life' we read that, at first, he believed that he would be able to find his 'desert' place in the middle of the ocean, where he would be undisturbed in his devotions. After experiencing the vagaries of sea voyages, he changed his mind and set out instead to search for a Land of Promise, an earthly paradise in a new land, far away. His voyages took place around the middle of the 6th century, and he was a contemporary of Columba, Kentigern and Cadoc.
Brendan came from Kerry, where he was educated by Bishop Erc. He was anxious to find this Promised Land because he believed it would be deserted, and it would be a wonderful place for those seeking a desert place to be alone with Christ. He wanted it for himself, but also for all those young people in Ireland who were finding life difficult in what was becoming a crowded island.
He travelled with a young disciple called Malo, and they set sail with a fleet of large curraghs, made of oxhide and wood, each carrying 30 to 40 men apiece. His first voyage took them to the Faroe islands but, realising that the boats were not strong enough to cope with the huge Atlantic waves, they returned to Ireland where

Brendan sought out shipwrights and workmen to build larger and sturdier boats. These workmen agreed to build the new boats with no wages, but on condition that they could be among the crews on the next adventure.

On the next journey, Brendan and his party reached Iceland and from Iceland, he then travelled to Newfoundland which he recognised immediately as the Land of Promise he had been searching for. There is a story that he was prevented from settling, or even exploring, this new land, as he had a vision of a young man who told him that, yes, indeed, this was the land he was seeking. But God wanted him to return home and tell people about it, so that the Christians would know that there was a land they could escape to, when the time of great persecution of Christians took place, in the years to come.

Brendan and Malo did return home. Perhaps some of the crews remained in Iceland or the Faroes as there is evidence of Irish occupation around the coasts in both areas, dating back before the Norse invasions in the 10th century. It is likely that Brendan's voyages encouraged travellers and that the journeys, to and from Ireland and these distant places, became commonplace.

Brendan continued to sail and found churches around the Irish and Scottish coasts but when he was old he gave up his strenuous sea journeys and retired to Clonfert and,with his disciple Malo, travelled to Brittany and settled there.

In 1976 the famous British explorer,Tim Severin, decided to repeat Brendan's trip in an oxhide curragh of the same size used by Brendan on his trip. The boat was 36 foot long with two masts and was made of Irish oak and ash, and wascompletedly cocooned in sheets of tanned ox-hide and fastened together by leather thongs. He sailed from Ireland to Peckford Island, Newfoundland, a distance of 4,500 miles. On the way he visited all the places mentioned in Brendan's 'life'. Brendan described what he saw and, of course, the places were not named. Severin wanted to see if the details of the journey were accurate, by identifying the places by the descriptions. He believed that the 'Islands of Sheep ' were probably the Faroes, 'the mountains that pelted the travellers with hot stones' were the volcanoes of southern Iceland, the 'pillars of crystal' were the floating icebergs and 'the thick fog' which Brendan describes just before reaching the Land of Promise was the almost perpetual fog bank which occurs to the east of Newfoundland. Tim Severin took 14 months to complete the journey, because, like Brendan, he stopped for a while at all the places mentioned in Brendan's 'life'.

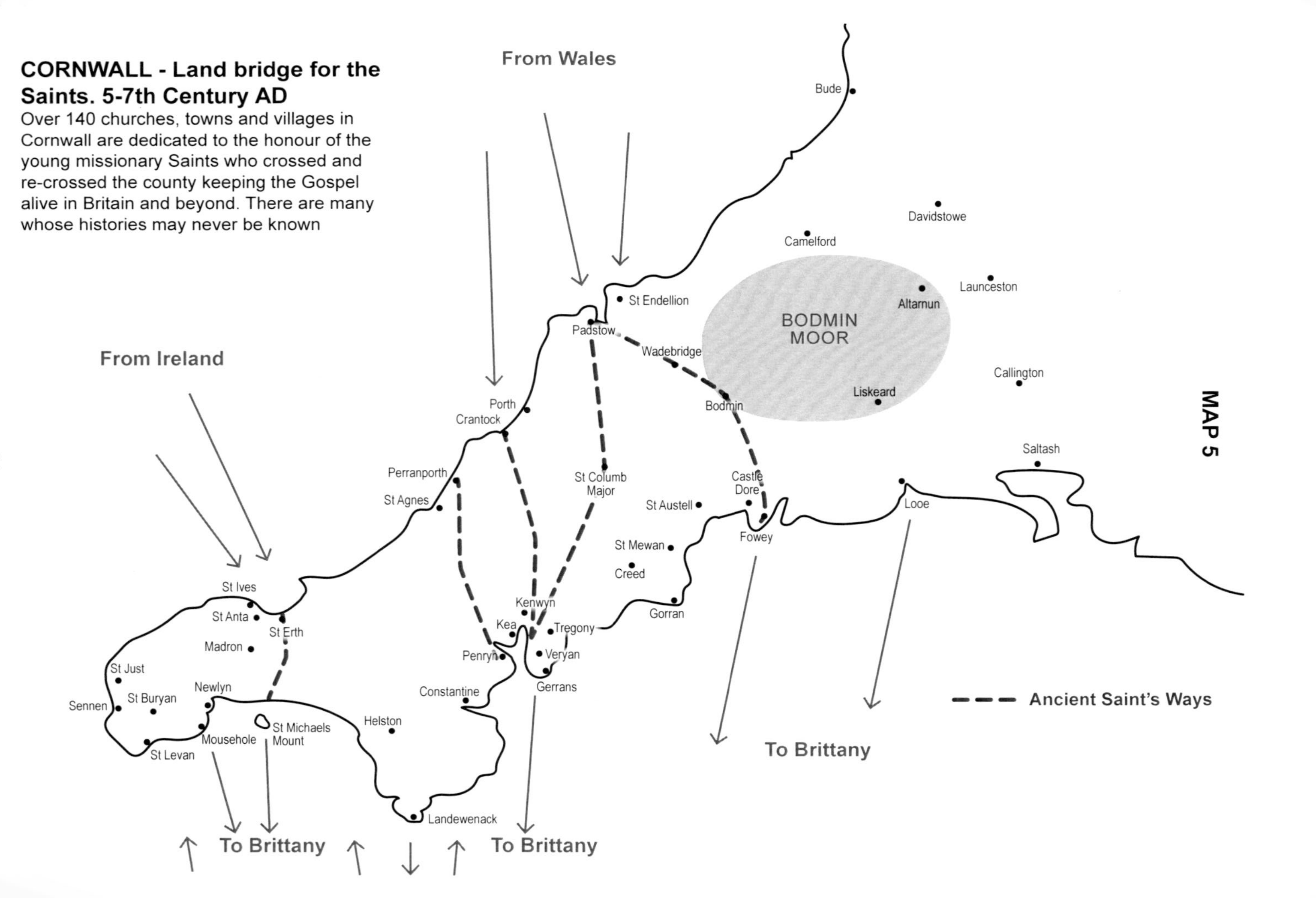
MAP 5
CORNWALL - Land bridge for the Saints. 5-7th Century AD
Over 140 churches, towns and villages in Cornwall are dedicated to the honour of the young missionary Saints who crossed and re-crossed the county keeping the Gospel alive in Britain and beyond. There are many whose histories may never be known
From Wales
From Ireland
Bude
Davidstowe
Camelford
Launceston
Altarnun
BODMIN MOOR
Callington
Liskeard
St Endellion
Padstow
Wadebridge
Bodmin
Saltash
Porth
Crantock
Perranporth
St Agnes
St Columb Major
Castle Dore
St Austell
Looe
Fowey
St Mewan
Creed
Gorran
Kenwyn
Kea
Tregony
Veryan
Penryn
Gerrans
Constantine
St Ives
St Anta
St Erth
Madron
St Just
Newlyn
St Buryan
Sennen
Helston
St Michaels Mount
Mousehole
St Levan
Landewenack
Ancient Saint's Ways
To Brittany
To Brittany
To Brittany

The travels of Columbanus 7th Century AD

MAP 6

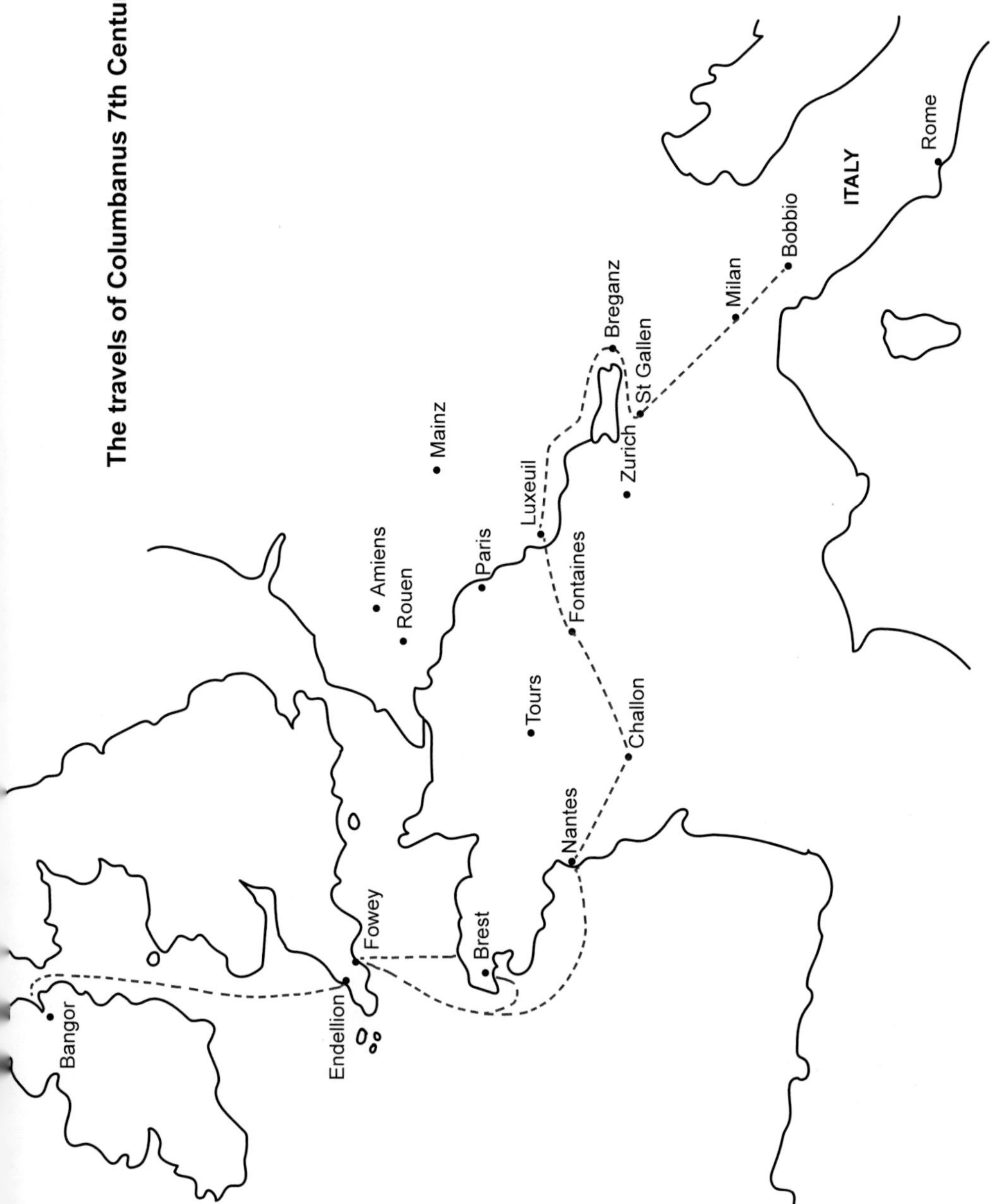

Bangor
Endellion
Fowey
Brest
Nantes
Tours
Challon
Fontaines
Amiens
Rouen
Paris
Mainz
Luxeuil
Zurich
St Gallen
Breganz
Milan
Bobbio
ITALY
Rome

CHAPTER TWELVE

Columba

Perhaps the most famous of all the monks in Ireland was Columba, who lived from AD 521-597. He was of royal birth, born into the tribe of the Ui Neill, at Gearten in Donegal, and became a monk at an early age. He was ordained deacon when he was 20 at the monastery of Finnian of Moville and, later, he was priested by his cousin Bishop Erchan. He founded his first monastery in Derry, on land given to him by his family, and, as his confidence and his contacts grew, he founded several more monasteries and had a mountain retreat at Glencolumkille, in Donegal.

As a young man he was larger than life and tempestuous. He was frequently argumentative and, rarely wishing to acknowledge that the fault might be his, he even managed to argue with the most placid and revered of monks, the saintly Ciaran. When Ciaran died, Columba was still shifting the blame for the bad feeling between them, and he is reported as saying, "Blessed is God who called Ciaran from this world in his youth. If he had lived to old age, he would have aroused many men's hostility."

Once, when visiting Finnian, he borrowed a psalter from Finnian's library and secretly copied it at night. When he had almost finished, he was discovered, and Finnian angrily demanded both the psalter and the copy back. Columba handed back the psalter but refused to give Finnian the copy. Finnian took Columba to court, before the High King, who ruled in favour of Finnian, ordering Columba to return the copy. (This was the first known law suit concerning copyright). But Columba never did return the copy and kept it with him for the rest of his life.

Columba's personality and his royal birth made him popular with both parents and pupils, and the time came when he was abbot to the largest body of monks in Ireland, and, because of his position in his family, he also had control of the largest army in Ireland. In AD 561, the High King invaded Connaught after a royal hostage was killed, while under the protection of an abbot. Columba was pressed into battle and was called to say the prayers before the action started. He prayed for the success of his men. Finnian was called to pray for the opposing side. The slaughter was horrendous and the armies of the High King won. There then started a rumour that Columba had a greater influence with God and that his prayers were more powerful than those of other clergy. Not a reputation that was good for someone with an ego as big as Colomba's.

A synod was called and it was decided that Columba should be excommunicated, but Brendan intervened and persuaded the synod to change its mind. Columba was banished from Ireland instead and was challenged by the Abbot Lasrain, to go out into the world and " win more souls for Christ than you have caused to die in battle." Chastened, and with great sadness, Columba left Ireland and, in the company of 12 faithful monks, he sailed north towards Scotland. He took with him his copy of the psalter.

We know that he eventually settled at Iona, but first he had to get permission to do so. The voyage took him north to King Connall, the new king of Argyll, who, knowing of Columba's royal connections, agreed to give him the island of Iona. But this was not as simple as it seemed, because the island marked a boundary between Connall's kingdom and that of King Brude, and Brude believed the island belonged to him. Columba agreed to visit Brude, in Inverness, to try and negotiate a lasting peace between the two kings. It was a long journey (during which he saw the Loch Ness monster)* but he was successful. The peace lasted between the two kingdoms for 80 years and both kings agreed that Iona should be his. Colomba was about 50 when he arrived to settle on Iona and he lived until he was 76.

100 years before Columba went to Iona, an Irish monk, Odhrain, had lived there alone and Columba found the remains of his cell when he began to build. The island is two and a half miles long and at its widest point it is just over a mile. It lies less than a mile west of Mull, close enough for someone to call across the Sound when they needed picking up by boat, and a small island close to Mull is called 'the isle of women,' and is the site of a small nunnery which is thought to have existed during Columba's time.

Columba's 'life' was written by the ninth abbot of Iona named Adomnan. He obviously knew the island well for, as well as describing many of the journeys made by Columba to the different parts of Scotland, he paints an evocative word picture of life on the island in Columba's time. He tells us of the flock of sheep and the vegetable plots, and how the monks collected seaweed to dig into the thin soil to make it fertile. He describes how the monks made bread and how some of them built boats, while others built the huts to accommodate visitors. Other monks would travel to the mainland to fell trees and bring the wood back to the island to help with the building, still others would be working on copying books and illustrating manuscripts. And through it all Columba would walk with his white cowl over his head, encouraging

and cajoling, stopping to talk and sharing a laugh. His was definitely not an austere, strict monastery as had been the custom of many of the earlier foundations.
As time went on Columba travelled less. He was still sought for his advice, for he had mellowed and become a man of great humility and wisdom. Columba's school attracted students from all over the British Isles and Europe, and he himself became spiritual director and counsellor to many a royal personage. He had been so upset when he left Ireland that he never believed he could live happily anywhere else, but the poetry he left behind, expresses his intense love of his new life on Iona. It brought him happiness and peace.
In his old age, he took delight in working in the library, copying the scriptures. The psalm he was copying during his last days, was Psalm 33, the psalm which Jesus quoted on the cross before He died.
When Columba felt that the time of his death was near, the monks harnessed up his favourite white horse, and, placing him in a wagon, drove him slowly round the island so that he could say his goodbyes, and see that everything was in good order. Finally, that night, he went to the chapel before everyone else and collapsed at the altar. With his head resting on his servant, Diormit's, lap, he died while his monks chanted the night office, and when they had finished, they carried his body back to his hut. It was a wild, stormy night and mourners couldn't get across from Mull, so his monks grieved for him alone for three days. He was buried on his beloved island, with the sound of the wind and the sea and the sea birds crying, welcoming him home.

Columba's Rock.
Delightful it is to stand on the peak of the rock,
in the bosom of the isle,
Gazing on the face of the sea.

I hear the heaving waves chanting a tune to God
in heaven:
I see their glittering surf.

I see the golden beaches, the sands sparkling:
I hear the joyous shrieks of the swooping birds.

I hear the waves breaking, crashing on the rocks, like

thunder in heaven,
I see the mighty whales.

I watch the ebb and flow of the ocean tide: it
holds my secret.
My mournful flight from Eire.

Contrition fills my heart as I hear the sea. It chants
my sins,
sins too numerous to confess.

Let me bless almighty God, whose power extends
over sea and let,
whose angels watch over all.

Let me study sacred books to calm my soul:
I pray for peace
kneeling at heaven's gates

Let me do my daily work, gathering seaweed,
catching fish,
giving food to the poor.

Let me say my daily prayers, sometimes chanting,
sometimes quiet, always thanking God.

Delightful it is to live on a peaceful isle, in a quiet
cell,
serving the King of Kings.

St Colomba of Iona.

*The first recorded sighting of the Loch Ness monster. The date was 563.AD

CHAPTER THIRTEEN

Christianity reaches Northumbria

Because of his royal background, Columba was comfortable and at ease when talking to kings and nobles. He understood how they thought and knew instinctively how to gain their trust. His dealings with the Gallic speaking King Connal of Dalriada and the Pictish King Brude of Inverness led to peace between the two men, a peace which lasted long after Columba's death. He also understood, only too well, that it was necessary to get the kings and nobles on side, if a mission in their lands had any chance of success. So it was that Columba would offer a hand of friendship to the leaders of the pagan lands, and when the contact had been made and cemented, he would send in his teams of missionaries. As a result, monks from Iona travelled all over Scotland and northern England, preaching the Gospel and founding monasteries.

Relationships between the lands of Northumbria and the middle England land of Mercia were volatile. Originally part of Celtic British Northumbria, both had been invaded by Angles from Denmark and were ruled by the Danish King Ida from his capital at Bamburgh. Around AD 626, Ida's cousin, Penda, rebelled and Mercia broke away from Northumbria becoming, under Enda's rule, an independent and powerful kingdom. Ida was a Christian and allowed the missionaries from Ireland to evangelise in his lands, whereas Penda remained a pagan all his life. This not to say that there were no Christians in Mercia, because, of course, there were many of the original British families who still kept the faith. Over a period of about 40 years there were invasions and counter attacks, which meant that there was no peace between the two lands.

In Northumbria, Ida was deposed by his brother Edwin who made an alliance with the king of Kent to marry his daughter Ethelburga. Ethelburga was a Christian and part of the agreement was that Edwin, who had been brought up as a Christian but who had not taken his faith seriously, would become a Christian too. Ethelburga travelled north with her chaplain, Paulinus, and Edwin and his entire court, converted and were baptised.

Unfortunately, a few years later, Edwin was killed at the battle of Hatfield Chase and Northumbria was ravaged by both Penda and the British King Cadwallon, and was nearly brought to its knees. Ethelburga and Paulinus fled back to Kent, and Edwin's

two nephews,(Ida's sons) fled to Iona where they were educated in safety.
When the two brothers eventually returned to Northumbria, one was killed but the other, Oswald, survived and led a rebellion against Cadwallon and Penda and managed to push them south, out of his lands. He then sent a message to Iona asking the abbot to send a bishop, to help him convert the people of Northumbria.
The abbot responded by sending his most experienced churchman, a monk named Colman. Colman's mission did not go well. He was too strict and demanded too much and the Northumbrians voted with their feet. A frustrated Colman returned to Iona, complaining of an "obstinate and barbarous people."
The abbot tried again, this time sending a gentle and patient monk named Aidan and 12 disciples. Oswald knew him well from his student days, and was delighted. He gave Aidan the island of Lindisfarne to be the seat of his new see and, because Aidan didn't speak English, he agreed to accompany him as he travelled around teaching. The two men enjoyed each other's company, and the people were moved to see how their king treated their new bishop with such respect, and many were converted.
Aidan turned Lindisfarne into a monastic community along the lines of Iona and many of the wealthy families begged him to take their sons as pupils. He was given money, but, instead of using the money to improve the living conditions, he used it, instead, to buy slaves and free them. Many of the slaves, who were unable to return to their families, joined the monastery as monks and were educated and taught skills. He also established monasteries at Tynemouth, Barrow and Lastingham.
Unfortunately Oswald was killed in battle by Penda in AD 642 near present day Oswestry, and was succeeded by his brother,Oswy, who shared the throne of Northumbria with Edwin's nephew Oswin. After Oswald's death, 62 churches were dedicated to him, and, although educated at Iona in the Celtic Christian tradition, he had been baptised as a child by Paulinus and thus was qualified to be considered a Christian of the Roman tradition and as a result he could be made a saint.
His saint's day is on August 9th.
Oswin continued to support Aidan's work and is remembered, particularly, for giving the ageing Aidan a horse to help him travel round the kingdom. Aidan took the horse, with many thanks, and then gave it to the first poor man he met along the way. Aidan dearly loved the gentle, kindly young Oswin and was sad because he knew that Oswin would never survive in the harsh world of violent politics. He was right to be anxious: Oswy, unable to cope with sharing the throne, arranged for the murder of Oswin, in the August of AD 651.
Aidan died 11 days later and his body was taken back to Lindisfarne for burial.

The next Bishop of Lindisfarne was Finan, an Irish monk who had accompanied Aidan from Iona. Finan sent missionaries into Mercia. Penda had died and had been succeeded by his son Peada,who was converted by Finan, and who asked him to send bishops into the kingdom. Finan sent two brothers, Cedd and Chad. They were two of four brothers who had been sent to Lindisfarne to school. They had been taught by Aidan and all four of the young men had spent time at monasteries in Ireland and had done missionary work in Scotland. In AD 653 Cedd began preaching in Mercia and then moved to Essex. He founded monasteries at Tilbury and at Bradwell on Sea, near Colchester.

On a home visit to Northumbria he acted as translator at the Council of Whitby in AD 664.

While Finan was bishop at Lindisfarne, Bede tells us that he built a church on the island, "suitable for an episcopal see." The church was built of hewn oak, thatched with reeds in the style of the Celtic church. But Eadbert, a later Bishop of Lindisfarne, removed the thatch and covered both roof and walls with sheets of lead.

CHAPTER FOURTEEN

The Council of Whitby

Oswy was a shrewd leader. Skilled in the art of diplomacy, his first option was always to try and make friends with the kings and leaders of the lands around him. Sigbert, the pagan king of East Sussex became a firm friend and, at their jovial meetings, Oswy would often tease Sigbert
about his worship of gods made of wood or stone. This gentle teasing allowed Oswy to tell Sigbert about a creator god who was powerful enough to do marvellous things, and it was not long before Sigbert, and his Mercian kingdom, were asking for bishops to teach them the Christian faith.

Oswy lived a busy life of constant battles and urgent matters of diplomacy. He had a quick mind and enjoyed the cut and thrust of debate. He was to be particularly remembered for having called together the great synod at Whitby in AD 664.

Oswy had been taught his Christian faith by the Celtic monks who had comefrom Iona, but his wife, Queen Eanfled, had been tutored by monks from Kent who had, in their turn, received the Gospel from St Augustine of Canterbury. In his own home, Oswy encountered the two branches of the Christian church in Britain, and it didn't make for harmony. The problem was the date of Easter. The Celtic Church kept Easter on the 14th day of the 3rd month, whereas the established Roman Church had it as a moveable feast which depended on the full Passover moon and the day of the week. Frequently, grumbled Oswy, he had just finished 40 days of Lenten fast and was looking forward to feasting at Easter, when the whole household was plunged into gloom again, because his wife and servants were then starting their Lenten fast. It was too much for a man to take!

Determined to sort out the problem, Oswy invited bishops and scholars from both side of the argument to meet him at the monastery at Whitby, so that a decision could be made.

Whitby was a dual monastery, for both men and women, and it was run very efficiently by the Abbess Hilda. Hilda had been a great friend of Bishop Aidan, and Whitby was a Celtic foundation.

Oswy was strongly in favour of the Celtic way, but his son Alchfrid, who had studied Christian doctrine in Rome, favoured the Roman way. Both father and son attended the synod, as did Bishop Colman and his Celtic clergy and Bishop Agilbert with two Roman priests, named Agatho and Wilfred. Bishop Cedd was present as translator and he and Hilda strongly supported the Celtic way.

King Oswy opened the proceedings by saying that, as they were all hoping, one day, to enter together into the Kingdom of Heaven, it was only right that there should be no differences between them, and that when everyone had listened to the arguments and a vote had been taken, the decision would be graciously accepted and binding upon them all. He then asked Colman to speak first.
Colman stood up and explained that the custom of the dating of Easter had been passed down through the years and originated from the evangelist and beloved disciple, St.John. It was St,John's dating which the Celtic Church followed.
Wilfred was asked to speak to the counter argument and said that the mainstream, Roman church had, from the very beginning, observed the dating of Easter as set down by St.Peter in Rome before he died. He also argued that this dating was used by Christians all over the world and "the only people who stupidly contend against the whole world are these Scots (Irish) and their partners in obstinacy, the Picts and the Britons, who inhabit only a portion of the two uttermost islands of the ocean."
Colman immediately got to his feet and said that it was strange that Wilfred should call them 'stupid' when they were faithfully keeping the customs handed down by the Apostle John who was counted worthy to sit beside our Lord and lay his head upon his breast.
Wilfred said that he wasn't calling St John 'stupid' but that John's words had been wilfully misinterpreted. He then explained, in intricate detail, where the Celtic church had gone wrong in its calculations and ended by saying that they were not even following John's dates accurately, and as they were deliberately disobeying Peter's instructions, they were guilty of sin.
Colman tried to argue further, but Wilfred was a skilful debater and pressed home his main point,
"do you imagine that a few men in a corner of a remote island, are to be preferred before the universal Church of Christ throughout the world? And even if your Columba – or may I say, ours also if he was the servant of Christ – was a saint potent in miracles, can he take precedence before the most blessed Prince of the Apostles, to whom our Lord said ' Thou art Peter, and upon this rock I will build my Church, and the gates of hell shall not prevail against it, and I will give unto thee the keys to the kingdom of heaven?'"
Oswy, who had been listening intently asked, "Is it true, Colman, that these words were spoken to that Peter by our Lord?" "It is true, your majesty." Colman answered. Oswy then asked if Columba had received similar authority and when Colman had to admit that he hadn't, Oswy then gave his verdict

"Then I tell you," he said "Peter is guardian of the Gates of Heaven, and I shall not contradict him. I shall obey his commands in everything to the best of my knowledge and ability, otherwise, when I come to the gates of heaven, there may be no one to open them, because he who holds the key has turned away."

From that day onwards all the monasteries and churches in Northumbria and Mercia fell in line with the Roman Church and celebrated Easter on the same day. All the monks and priests in the two kingdoms, whose hair was cut in the same way as St Martin, long at the back and shaved in the front from ear to ear, also grew their hair into the round Roman tonsure. The monasteries grew more substantial and were built of stone, and the monks began to live as members of a community, rather than in individual cells. The austere Celtic way began to be replaced with the more moderate Benedictine rule. In Wales, Dumnonia and Ireland it took longer for the churches to toe the line but, over time, and with more peaceful times allowing the possibility of travel once again, it happened eventually.

After the Synod Colman returned to Iona and Iata, a pupil of Aidan, became Abbot at Lindisfarne. When Colman left he took with him all those monks who had decided not to stay and submit to the new rules, and he took most of the bones of Aidan to bury on the island. A few bones were left at Lindisfarne, the place of Aidan's mission. But, when Colman left, Bede says that there was hardly any trace of a Celtic monastic foundation to be seen, except the little church. From Aidan's time until Colman, the monks had lived so frugally, that once they were gone, they left very few traces behind them.

Cedd, who had been translator for the synod, was the eldest of four brothers who attended Aidan's school at Lindisfarne. The boys were named Cedd, Caelin, Cynibil and Chad.

Cedd had worked as a missionary in East Sussex and was consecrated as bishop by Finan. He was a brilliant preacher and converted many people to Christ. In Essex he built a monastery at Tilbury but on a visit home to Northumbria he was given land by the king and built another monastery at Lastingham with the help of his brother Caelin. In his later years he bequeathed Lastingham to his brother Chad.

When Cedd had been bishop for many years he went back to the monastery on a pastoral visit, but, unfortunately the monks had fallen sick because of the plague and Cedd, too, became ill and died. When the monks at Tilbury heard that their beloved Father in God had died at Lastingham, 30 of them journeyed to his resting place. They were welcomed by the monks and chose to stay close to the tomb of Cedd. Unfortunately the plague had not run its course, and all of them died.

Agricultural records of the time tell us that in AD 664 there was a great drought accompanied by plague which spread through the land and which lasted on and off for the next 23 years.

In AD 665, Oswy's son, Alchfrid, sent Chad to Canterbury to be consecrated bishop. The archbishop had unexpectedly died, so Chad went into Wessex and was consecrated bishop by Bishop Winni, with the assistance of two British bishops. He returned to Northumbria and was given Ripon as the seat of his episcopal see. But Wilfred protested and insisted that he should be consecrated again as two of the three bishops at his consecration were not in communion with Rome. Chad submitted to this correction with great humility. In all things Chad chose to emulate his old teacher Aidan. He lived humbly, walking everywhere and spending his time visiting the poor. In AD 672 he retired to his monastery at Lastingham and on one occasion, when all the brothers were in the church, except one lay brother called Owinni, who was working outside in the garden, Chad was in his room reading. Owinni said later that he saw a wondrous light and heard beautiful singing coming from Chad's room. When he asked Chad what it was that he had heard, Chad told him that the angels had come to tell him that in seven days he would die and that heaven was waiting to welcome him. He urged him not to tell anyone until after his death. The next day Chad became ill of the plague and grew steadily worse, and, as the angels had foretold, he died on the seventh day. Many miracles were recorded by those who visited his tomb and his relics were translated to Lichfield in AD 1148.

Bede records that when the Abbess Hilda died, a nun called Begu in the monastery at Hackness, some miles away, was awakened by the ringing of a bell. She opened her eyes and saw the roof open and in the dazzling light, she saw Hilda being led up to heaven, guided by angels. She ran to wake the prioress who gathered the sisters and offered prayers for Hilda's soul. In the morning the brothers came from the men's monastery to give them the news, only to be told that the nuns already knew.

In AD 685 King Egfrid of Northumbria appointed the revered and elderly Cuthbert as Bishop of Lindisfarne. He was the gentlest and simplest of men. He entered the monastery of Melrose while he was still a young man, and was made prior when the elderly prior, Boisil, died. Cuthbert was a wonderful preacher and people came from miles around to listen to him. He was humble and kind and spent hours with the poor, often going to the mountains to meet with tribes people who lived in abject poverty, away from the towns and civilisation. Eventually, Abbot Eata transferred him to Lindisfarne. At Lindisfarne Cuthbert allowed his longing for a 'desert' place, where he could be alone with Christ, to come to the fore. He found his place, close by, on the little island of Farne. He told his monks that if it was not God's will for him to live on Farne, he would soon know and that he would then return to be with them again.

The island had no water, no trees and no corn. But when Cuthbert arrived there he prayed earnestly and told the monks who had taken him there by boat, to dig a hole, and, when they did, he found a spring of water. He built himself a cell of stones and a small church and then a wall of stones completely all around him, to keep out the wind and the sea. The wall was so high that he could only see the sky. He had a supply of farming implements and a store of wheat, but the wheat failed badly, so the next year he planted barley which did well.

Cuthbert stayed on Farne for many years, but eventually, at an important synod, everyone voted that Cuthbert should be consecrated Bishop of Lindisfarne. Cuthbert was horrified. He had hoped to stay alone on Farne until he died, but those who were sent to fetch him were moved to tears in their pleading and, in the end, Cuthbert, also in tears, went with them back to Lindisfarne.

As a bishop, Cuthbert acquitted himself well. People were impressed by his holiness and his constant prayer and his excellent teaching. Bede says that, "Like a good teacher, he taught others to do only what he first practised himself. Above all else, he was afire with heavenly love, unassumingly patient, devoted to unceasing prayer, and kindly to all who came to him for comfort."

After two years as Bishop, Cuthbert returned to Farne and lived out his last days as the hermit he always wanted to be. He hoped he could be buried on the island but gave in to the arguments of his brothers and agreed that they could take his body back to Lindisfarne. The year of his death was AD 687.

Now long dead, all the young saints who had followed Antony, Martin, Pelagius, and the teachers of the refugee Britons in Wales, Dumnonia, Brittany, Ireland, Iona, Scotland and Northumbria, would have identified with Cuthbert and recognised the joys and the sorrows of his life. They each had the same ties and the same challenges. Most were from noble families and had chosen to give up comfort, wealth, position and power in order to live as Christ lived, as someone who had "nowhere to lay his head." They all longed for the 'desert' place, but people needed them and they were constantly torn between duty and desire.

The historian Bede did not agree with the theology of the Celtic Church. It was neither proper nor correct. To him, the Celtic bishops did not have the dignity of the bishops of the Roman Church. But all the same he couldn't help but be impressed. When Bishop Colman returned home to Iona, after the synod of Whitby, Bede graciously recorded these words

"So frugal and austere were Colman and his predecessors that when they left the seat of their authority there were very few buildings except the church; indeed, no more than met the bare requirements of a seemly way of life. They had no property except cattle, and whenever they received money from rich folk, they immediately gave it to the poor; for they had no need to amass money or provide lodgings for important people, since such visited the church only in order to pray or hear the word of God. Whenever opportunity offered, the king himself used to come with only five or six attendants; and when he had completed his prayers in the church, he used to leave. But if they happened to remain for a meal, they were content with the plain daily food of the brothers and asked for nothing more. For in those days the sole concern of these teachers was to serve God, not the world; to satisfy the soul, not the belly.

"Accordingly the religious habit at that time was held in high esteem. Wherever any priest or monk paid a visit, he was joyfully welcomed by all as the servant of God. And if people met him on the road, they ran to him and bowed, eager to be signed by his hand or receive a blessing from his lips. Whenever he spoke a word of encouragement, he was given an attentive hearing. On Sundays the people flocked to the churches and the monasteries, not to obtain food but to hear the word of God. When a priest visited a village, the people were quick to gather together to receive the word of life; for priests and clerics always came to a village solely to preach, baptise, visit the sick and, in short, to care for the souls of its people. They were so far from the sin of avarice that none of them would accept lands or gifts for the building of monasteries unless expressly directed to do so by the secular authorities. This continued to be the general practice for some years among the churches of the Northumbrians."

With this endorsement it would be possible to conclude our story. The ideas and the inspiration which drove this movement of young people started with Antony, and Martin in the 4th Century but it was the invasion of the Saxons in AD 442 and the evacuation of the British families which gave impetuous to these ideas, and opportunity to the teachers to make their dreams come true. If we take that moment in time as the start of the movement in Britain and measure it to the death of Cuthbert, we are only talking about a period of 245 years. Celtic Christianity was then slowly subsumed by the universal Roman Church, on the mainland of Britain. Some isolated monasteries hung on longer than others, but eventually the Celtic Church came to an end. What remained, however, was the British longing for a quiet place to be alone with Christ, a deep love of the natural world, the determination to show loving kindness to all, and the common sense ideas of their earliest theologian, the heretic Pelagius. So, as I say, this would be a good place to end, if it were not for the fact that the Church in Ireland was still determined to keep these ideas alive.

As we have seen, Ireland was firmly aligned with Rome and therefore the Church in Ireland was not considered to be in need of reform. But the monasteries of Ireland had been so strongly influenced by the Celtic Christian teachers, that their torch still burned as brightly as the fire outside Brigid's Church of the 'City of the Poor' in Kildare. The difference being that the torch now shone from inside the Roman Church and not just from the outside.

So, as this is obviously not quite the end, we will look at the story of just one more Irish saint who, living at a time when the Celtic Church was still active and flourishing, left Ireland and travelled to Europe. As he travelled he so inspired those he met on the way, that the seeds of the Celtic form of Christianity were planted, monasteries were built and hearts were, once again, enthused by the power of the Gospel.

CHAPTER FIFTEEN

Columbanus goes to Europe

Columbanus, whose name means 'white dove', was born in AD 542 in the southern county of Leinster in Ireland. He was the son of a single mother, a Christian, who lived in a close knit village community. As he was an only child, she was a loving but, perhaps, over protective mother. When other boys from the village were sent away to school or to other families to train as squires, she chose to educate Columbanus herself.

He was an intelligent boy and quickly learned all she had to teach and, realising that if Columbanus was going to do well in life, he would need to go to school. She enrolled him at the closest school so that he could continue to live at home. At school he would have been taught rhetoric, grammar, and geometry, and he would have been expected to spend much of his time studying the Holy Scriptures. Yet again, he proved to be an excellent student, outstripping the other students and even some of his teachers. He was also tall and good looking and, as time went on, he was tempted to spend more and more time with the girls. His teachers believed that he should join one of the monastic communities, become a monk and continue his studies. They foresaw a great academic future for him. His mother, not wanting him to leave her, hoped for a stable, local job and a good marriage. Columbanus, under pressure, took himself off for a long walk, to get away from his increasingly claustrophobic life and to think things out for himself.

As he walked further and further into the hills, he found a small hut and an elderly woman living there alone. She was an anchoress who spent her time in prayer and in contemplation of the Scriptures. Columbanus was fascinated and stopped to talk to her. She told him that, like many young people she had known, she had dreamed of taking on the white martyrdom, leaving her family and her home and travelling across the sea to take the Gospel to the pagans. But, when the moment came, she had lost her nerve and stayed at home. Now she was living the life of a hermit. She was content with her lot but she would always be ashamed of her cowardice. Then she looked at Columbanus and said, "But you, glowing with the fire of youth, stay quietly on your native soil; out of weakness you lend your ear even against your will, to the voice of the flesh, and think you can associate with the female sex without sin. Away, O youth! Away, flee from corruption!"

Columbanus was startled. She had jolted him out of the misery of his indecision. He realised that she was not a crazy old woman, as he had first thought. Instead she had to be very brave to live alone in the hills, and be very committed to live a life of such frugality and hardship. He admired her strength.

As he returned home, he made up his mind that he would leave to find a monastery where he could continue his studies and where he could experience a strict discipline and become equally as strong.

When he told his mother she was horrified and did all she could to prevent him leaving, but, fired by his new ambition, he walked away, leaving her crying alone.

Several new monasteries were being established and were looking for students. Columbanus walked north until he reached the island of Cleenish where the famous teacher, Sinell, had established a monastic school and, much to his relief, he was accepted as a student. For the next few years Columbanus was steeped in his studies and in monastic life. He learnt discipline and obedience and, following the daily cycle of prayers, he grew ever closer to Christ. He realised that he had made the right choice but he felt that life at Cleenish was too gentle, and longed to stretch himself still further and experience true austerity and even stricter discipline.

Cleenish had many visitors and, from them, Columbanus heard about the monastery at Bangor which had been founded ten years previously by the Abbot Comgall. Columbanus obtained Sinell's permission and travelled eagerly east to Bangor.

Comgall's foundation was large and supported a couple of hundred monks and students. It was made up of a large number of round wattle huts, several small wooden chapels, workshops, school rooms and kitchens, all surrounded by a large ditch and wall. Columbanus revelled in the discipline which was required of him; the frugal meals, the absolute obedience and the long hours of hard labour and study. It was not long before he was trusted with the teaching of some of the younger students and, after a while, some parents began asking for him by name to be their sons' teacher. In this way he met a young student called Gall who was to become his lifelong companion.

Columbanus stayed at Bangor until he turned 40. He had been a faithful, obedient member of the community. Several years earlier he had been priested and he had been content with the life he had chosen. But around the year AD 585 he began to think of the old woman and her dream of travelling overseas, and he was filled with a yearning to move on and take up the white martyrdom.

Comgall was reluctant to lose him but, after a while, he agreed and giving Columbanus 12 men (including young Gall) to accompany him, and enough provisions for the first days, he gave the monks his blessing and sent them on their way.

The boat they used was probably similar to Brendan's curragh, with oars and two sails. According to Jonas, who wrote Columbanus' life some years later, the seas were calm for the duration of this first voyage and they took two days to reach the north Cornish coast and landed at a small bay close to Padstow. Making their way to a small monastic settlement at St Endellion Columbanus asked the abbot if they could stay for a while.The abbot recognised Columbanus and had heard of his reputation as a strict disciplinarian and was fearful. He begged forgiveness for his lack of hospitality but asked Columbanus not to stay as he was afraid the great man would find the ways of his Cornish monks too lax and would be offended. As it was, Columbanus was eager to get on with his journey, and, leaving their boat behind them, he and his monks walked overland to Fowey in order to find a ship to take them to Brittany.

It is not certain if Columbanus was expecting to stay in Brittany as most of the young saints had done before him, but, although he spent time exploring the new land, he didn't find it to his liking. Too many holy men had come this way before. There were monasteries and churches everywhere. He had dreamed of taking the Gospel to the heathen, and it seemed that he would not be needed in Brittany, so he and his party moved on into France which turned out to be a more promising location. The old kingdom of the Gauls had been decimated by a Frankish invasion and all was chaos and confusion. It was an unhappy nation.

Columbanus and his men travelled around from village to village, preaching and bringing words of comfort. Although it had been a long time since the days of St Martin, the people had heard stories of the great bishop and his disciples, so the strange tonsure of Colombanus and his disciples and their austere appearance did not seem so strange to the country people around Tours, and as they journeyed so their reputation increased.The Frankish King Guntram at his court in Chalon, received news of them and sent messengers to summon them to his court. Without question, they left at once and arrived in Chalon six days later.

King Guntram was immediately impressed by the educated, sophisticated but rather stern Columbanus. The two men talked for hours and once they discovered that each shared a love of music, they became firm friends. Guntram hoped that Columbanus would consider becoming a personal adviser to him and his court. Life would be so much easier with a capable man like Columbanus at his side. Columbanus hesitated. He knew that between them the two men could make a real difference but he thought of the old lady and the way she had turned her back on a secular life and once putting her hand to the plough, there had been no turning back. Seeing his dilemma, Guntram kindly offered him something different. "Stay in France where you are needed," he told him, "and make your hermitage here." This was an offer

Columbanus could not refuse.

Columbanus found a derelict, abandoned Roman estate which suited his purpose very well and he and his men began the work to build the church, the cells and the school room, and toiled long hours clearing the land and preparing it for sowing. This first foundation in France was at Annegray. It was a pretty spot and had been popular with the Romans in the past. When the first winter came, however, there was not enough from their first harvest to carry them through the cold months and the men became ill. They decided that it was time for urgent prayers, and Heaven was assaulted for three whole days and nights. On the third day a farmer called Marculf, arrived with a wagon of food. Apparently the Breton abbot of a monastery at Salicis had had a dream in which he was told to send food to the monks at Annegray. He asked one of his farmers to set off with a wagon full of food, but the farmer became totally lost. He felt inadequate, but, deciding that if God wanted the food delivered He could show the horses which way to go. So he let go of the reins and gave the horses their head. They led him straight to Annegray. The brothers recovered and the monastery went from strength to strength and the confused farmer told so many people about the incident, that people flocked to Columbanus to ask for prayers and for healing. Annegray was no longer a desert place and Columbanus was forced to look for an isolated cave in the nearby mountains where he could go when he needed to be alone. The cave he found was almost inaccessible, which is just how he liked it, and he began spending more and more of his time alone, with the birds and animals as his only company.
As so many young men were coming to the monastery at Annegray wanting to become monks, it became necessary to create a new foundation. Childebert gave Columbanus permission to build another monastery, and this he did at Luxeuil, a few miles north of Annegray. Luxeuil grew rapidly, and it became necessary, once more, to create a further foundation at Fontaine. Luxeuil was, by far, the largest of the three monasteries and became known as the mother house. Columbanus spent a great deal of time going from one to the other so he decided to write a 'rule' for all the monks to observe. The three monasteries were all run on the strict Celtic lines but each monk had chosen to join because he had wanted the more ascetic way of living. Many of the rules, therefore, were concerned with making sure that the monks did not practise their ascetic observances to dangerous extremes. The things which disturbed Columbanus the most were gossiping and slandering, and the punishment for these involved periods of fasting. Arguing could result in 50 blows from a leather

strap. Still, young men continued to come and nobles came to find counsel, and Columbanus was held in high esteem. Except, perhaps, in the eyes of a few of the older churchmen of the struggling old Gaulish Church.

They objected to Columbanus' use of the Celtic dating of Easter! Columbanus, proud of the Irish Celtic foundations he had been brought up to observe, had kept the old tradition going. He was summoned to a synod to explain himself, but decided not to attend and sent a letter instead, saying that he was nervous of attending for fear he would lose his temper with them all. It is not known how the problem was finally resolved, but it was not spoken of again.

A more serious problem began to come to the fore. Childebert died young and his land was divided into three distinct areas, and in AD 596 Guntram's cousin, Lothar, and Childebert's two young sons, Theuderbert and Theudoric, reigned in his stead, with his mother, Brunhilda, as regent.

Frustrated by Theudoric's admiration for Columbanus and by the fact that Theudoric preferred to take advice from Columbanus, rather than from his grandmother, Brunhilda decided to get rid of the Irish monk. In the end she succeeded and Columbanus was ordered to leave Burgandy and take his original disciples with him. His three foundations could remain intact and be run by trusted older monks, but Columbanus must go.

Under close arrest, and accompanied by Brunhilda's soldiers, Columbanus and his Irish companions were taken by boat, down to Nantes and then on to the coast. The journey took several very uncomfortable days and when they reached the coast, they were put on a ship to Ireland and the soldiers thankfully left them and returned home. As the ship left the river estuary to go out to sea, the wind got up and a large wave rolled in and carried the ship back inland and deposited it on the mud banks. When Columbanus decided to take a chance and escape, the Irish captain did not stop them. He was glad to see them go, as he had decided that these Irish monks were serious trouble, worse even than the Old Testament Jonah.

Taking a still further risk, the men walked into Neustria where the young king Lothar was reigning. It was a risk worth taking. Lothar remembered meeting Columbanus when he went with his father to Annegray, and he was delighted to see him. Columbanus was now 69, and he was glad to be offered sanctuary at Lothar's court. They stayed with Lothar for about four years, but, by then Columbanus was ready for his next adventure. He wanted to go to Italy and, if possible, Rome, before he was too old to make the journey. Unwilling to take the easier route which went through lands ruled over by Theudoric and Brunhilda, he had decided to go up the Rhine and

over the Alps.
Lothar did what he could to persuade him not to leave, but Columbanus was determined and in August of AD 610, accompanied by a royal escort to guide them for part of the way, they started on their last great adventure.
To get to the Alps they had, first, to travel through lands ruled over by Theuderbert, but they needn't have worried . Theuderbert remembered Columbanus kindly and was glad to see him. He knew full well how difficult his grandmother could be and was anxious to make amends. He told Columbanus that he owned land by the lakeside, over the border in Switzerland, which he would happily give to him if he thought it was what he wanted. He also gave the Irish monks a new boat and a team of rowers to assist them on the way. It was well that he did so because, after a few days, at a join in the river, they needed to row upstream, and the monks would never have had the strength to manage it.
After rowing upstream for several days they finally arrived at Mainz. Their food had completely run out and Columbanus took it upon himself to go into town and find supplies. He went straight to the church and lay, face down, with his arms outstretched in front of the altar, and prayed.
After a short while the bishop walked into his church and found Columbanus there. Columbanus told him that he and his monks had run out of food, and the bishop told him to go to his house and help himself to whatever he needed. Columbanus went back for the men and they took what they needed. After they had gone the bishop couldn't believe what had happened. He had never been so generous to anyone before, but his words had come out of his mouth before he could stop them. And afterwards he would laugh about it and say that one moment there was one man wanting food and, before he knew it, a whole string of monks were walking into his kitchen helping themselves!

The next part of the journey was long and tedious but then, suddenly, the journey became much harder, as they continued upstream. The river became narrower and faster and the cliffs became precipitous. They were really glad of Theuderbert's rowers, but when they suddenly emerged from the mountain passes and saw ahead of them a glassy lake, the rowers took their leave of them and started the long journey home. Unfortunately for Columbanus, they had taken a wrong turning somewhere on the route, and they had found the wrong lake. They might have stayed but the native tribes were unfriendly, and so they took to a mountain track and climbed away to see if they could find the land Theuderbert had given them. After several days, they did indeed find another lake and to their delight they found an old church and an old priest who came to greet them with arms outstretched. He told them that he had been struggling alone for so long that he had almost given up. He was so glad to see them and, when Gall preached at the first service in the church, he was so moved by Gall's words that he burst into tears. Across the lake they discovered the ruins of the old Roman city of Brigantium (Bregenz) and it seemed to be the ideal place to start their next monastery. Helped by the elderly priest, they began to build again, but, as soon as they had finished, trouble started. A local duke objected to the monks walking in the hills disturbing the game, and his men killed two of the monks claiming that they were trespassing. The community was devastated.

Then came the news that the two brothers, Theuderbert and Theudoric, had gone to war and that Theuderbert had been defeated and then killed by his Grandmother. Theudoric and Brunhilda took over his lands and were now rulers of much of the Frankish Kingdom, including the land on which the monks were now building. Almost immediately, the local duke appeared and told them that he had orders to remove Columbanus and his men from the land altogether. The monks were in utter despair. But Columbanus was quite calm, he knew that nothing now could stop him fulfilling his dream of going to Italy.

Once again the monks began to pack. It was going to be a long walk and, just as they were ready to leave, Gall fell sick and begged Columbanus to go on without him. Strangely Columbanus didn't believe him and, thinking that Gall was faking, he was quite stern with his best friend. When they walked away, Gall struggled to reach the home of the old priest, who nursed him back to health. Gall never saw his friend Columbanus again.

In the meantime, Columbanus and his Irish monks were climbing the Alps. They had to go up before they could come down the other side, and it was hard. But they were tough, and they reached Italy at last and took the road to Milan. In Milan, Columbanus was feted by the church heirarchy. His reputation had gone before him and they asked him to teach their best students and preach in their best churches and, perhaps best of all, he was invited to take part in the theological debates which were being held by the church elders.. He was flattered and enjoyed this new life but, in his heart, he knew he had to keep searching for his 'desert' place. King Agiluth of Milan, thought highly of him and when Columbanus confided in him that he wished to find somewhere to found a new monastery, the king promised to help him.

Land was found at Bobbio and Columbanus went to inspect it and found it to be perfect. The deeds were drawn up and Columbanus began, once more, to build.

Students began arriving before the buildings were finished and were encouraged to help. It didn't take long and a new monastery was soon up and running One of the first visitors was Eustasius, once one of his pupils, but now abbot of the three monasteries at Luxeuil. Columbanus was delighted to see him and to find out how the monasteries were faring. King Lothar had sent his regards, which also pleased him. He had heard that Lothar had patiently waited for the right moment and had then attacked Theoderic's army. Theudoric was killed in battle and Brunhilda had been tied to the tail of an unbroken horse and dragged to her death. Lothar was now King of the whole of the Frankish Kingdom..

Seeing that Columbanus was becoming old and frail, Eustacius begged him to return with him to Luxeuil and spend his last days in peace. Columbanus was tempted but the thought of the long journey unnerved him. There was too much to do in Bobbio and he decided to stay. He wrote a letter to Lothar and asked Eustacius to deliver it. No one knows what was in that letter. Congratulations perhaps, or condemnation for his treatment of his grandmother? No one will ever know.

Columbanus stayed at Bobbio. When he knew he was dying, his thoughts turned to his old friend Gall. He sent people to look for him and heard that he had recovered and had founded a small community in the Steinach Valley and was well respected for his fine preaching and his gift of healing. Columbanus gave orders that, when he died, his pastoral staff should be given to Gall. On Sunday 23rd November AD 615, Columbanus breathed his last. He was not alone in his 'desert' place as he thought he would be. Instead he was surrounded by those who cared for him, in the middle of a busy monastery which was buzzing with new life. The Celtic spirit had been kindled once again and who knew where it would travel next?

..ooOOOoo..

POSTSCRIPT

Throughout this brief history of the Celtic Church, we have concentrated mainly on what happened and when. I would like to conclude by drawing attention to the rather uniquely British way of thinking which formed a background to the religious aspirations of the Celtic saints. Even though the best of the teachers encouraged them to live in this world and not apart from it, many of the young and enthusiastic saints strove for perfection, by living austerely and in isolation. This was as true in Egypt as it was in Britain, and is true of many a young enthusiast today. But this asceticism was not the whole story. I mentioned the British theologian, Pelagius, in the first chapter. His letters give us a window into his thoughts and the thoughts of many British people of the time. Asceticism which led to perfection brought an inner joy to those who practised it, but it was not the only way.

Three Letters taken from The letters of Pelagius. *Celtic Soul Friend. edited by Robert Van de Weyer.*

To Demetrias.
Do not be deceived by those who seem to seek perfection, yet do not keep the basic commandments of God. There are people who eat little, who live simply and who are celibate; yet they show no love and compassion towards their neighbours. Before seeking perfection a person must first learn to love others and to be generous towards them. This world would be a most wonderful place if everyone was loving and generous: yet no one sought perfection; perfection is, as it were, a spiritual luxury, not a necessity. So even if you do aspire towards perfection, do not neglect the basic duties of love. If you see someone who is hungry, share your food. If you see someone who is thirsty, share your drink. If you see someone weeping, offer comfort. If you see someone in despair, offer hope. If you see someone utterly confused and bewildered, try to understand the confusion and then seek clarity. Unless you are loving and generous in these ways, seeking perfection is like trying to build a magnificent palace without putting in strong foundations.

To a new Christian.
When he walked from village to village speaking to the ordinary people he met, Jesus did not ask people to accept high-flown doctrines. In fact he did not ask them to

believe anything. Instead he asked them to enter into a relationship with God. He told them that if they prayed to God as a loving father, God would fill them with wisdom and strength. And he said that if they acted according to God's love, they would experience joy and peace in this life and the next. The proof of his teaching was his own example: through constant prayer he was supremely strong and wise; and by choosing to obey God in all things, he overflowed with joy. The proof too lay in the example of all those who followed his teaching. Do not let your mind be seduced by theological speculation; the human mind can never grasp the supreme glory of God. Simply follow Jesus wherever he leads.

To an elderly friend.
Look at the animals roaming the forest: God's spirit dwells within them. Look at the birds flying across the sky: God's spirit dwells within them. Look at the tiny insects crawling in the grass: God's spirit dwells within them. There is no creature on earth in whom God is absent. Travel across the ocean to the most distant land, and you will find God's spirit in the creatures there. Climb up the highest mountain, and you will find God's spirit among the creatures who live on the summit. When God pronounced that his creation was good, it was not only that his hand had fashioned every creature; it was that his breath had brought every creature to life. Look too at the great trees of the forest; look at the wild flowers and the grass in the field; look even at your crops. God's spirit is present in all plants as well. The presence of God's spirit in all living beings is what makes them beautiful; and if we look with God's eyes, nothing on the earth is ugly.

Source material...

Nennius, The History of the Britons (Historia Brittonum) Translated by J A Giles. Gutenburg's History. E book updated 2013. Nennius was a Welsh monk, living around 829. The authorship of The Historia Brittonum is attributed to him, but it is unlikely that he wrote it all (if any) as it shows several different styles of writing, and it appears to be an accumulation of manuscripts. The history concentrates on the stories of Vortigern, Vortimer and Arthur and appears to be remembered legend from Welsh traditional history, dating back to the 5th century.

Bede, A History of the English Church and People. Penguin Classics. Bede was born around 673 and was brought up as a child in monasteries in Jarrow. His history covers the period from the abortive arrival of Julius Caesar in 54BC and ends with the consecration of Tatwin as the 9th Archbishop of Canterbury in 731. It is the most comprehensive history of this period that we have. He also wrote 'The Life of St Cuthbert.' Bede died in Jarrow in 735.

Adomnan. Life of St. Columba, Penguin Classics. Adomnan was born in Ireland around 628. He was related to St Columba and in 679 he became the ninth abbot of Iona. He was a quiet, thoughtful man ,and he wrote 'the Life of Columba' on Iona. He died in 704.

Gildas. On the Ruin of Britain. (De Excidio Britanniae) Serenity Publishers. Rockville, Maryland. Gildas was born around 500. He was of royal birth and was sent for schooling to the teacher Illtyd. He was particular friends with Samson of Dol and Paul Aurelian. He began his travels by going north to Northumbria and after several years of missionary work he then travelled to Ireland and on to Brittany. He died in Rhuys in Brittany in 570. He wrote De Excidio Britanniae as a sermon in three parts, around 540. Other traditions tell us that he took an active part in the stories of Arthur and that he died in Glastonbury.

Jonas. The Life of St. Columban by the monk Jonas. D C Munro. 1895 reprint Llanerch Publishers. Jonas became a monk at Bobbio in Northern Italy three years after Columbanus' death in 615. He obtained his material from the elderly monks who had travelled with Columbanus from Ireland.

The Saints of Cornwall. Parts 1-6. Gilbert H Doble. Facsimile Reprint by Llanerch Publishers. Canon Gilbert Doble was born in Penzance in 1880. He graduated from Exeter College, Oxford and soon afterwards he attended Ely theological College and was priested in 1907. When he returned to Cornwall and became vicar at Wendron he spent a great deal of his time studying the Cornish Saints and translating their 'lives'. He died in 1977 and his personal library and his manuscripts are held in the Courtney library in the Royal Cornwall Museum. Truro.

The Age of Arthur. John Morris. Weidenfeld and Nicolson. London. John Morris was born in 1913 and read Modern History at Jesus College, Oxford. He served in the army during the Second World War and after the war he lectured at University College London and was Senior lecturer in Ancient History for twenty years before he died in 1977.

The Letters of Pelagius. Celtic Soul Friend. Ed. Robert Van de Weyer. Little Gidding Books.
Pelagius was born around 340, and the monastery he entered was thought to have been in North Wales. His Celtic name was Mawgan. He travelled to Rome where he became spiritual director to several important people. His letters show him to be a wise and kindly man with an attractive simplicity of thought. He challenged the ideas of St Augustine of Hippo and was excommunicated. He died a heretic in the Holy Land in 420.
Robert Van de Weyer has translated and edited his letters so well, that they are a joy to read.

USEFUL DATES

Antony in Egypt 251-356

Martin of Tours 372-397

Augustine of Hippo 386-430

Victricius visits Britain 396

Pelagius travels to Rome 400, dies 418

Sicillion Briton c 411

Britain independent 410

First British migration to Brittany 411

Germanus of Auxerre 418-448 (visits Britain 429 and 440)

Vortigern 425-459

Hengist and Horsa land in Kent 428

Patrick in Ireland 432-459

Cornovii sent to Cornwall 430

Severe plague 430

Saxons revolt 441

Famine and plague 447.

Second British migration to Brittany. 459

Ambrosius Aurelanius II succeeds Vortigern 460-475

Arthur 475-515

Illtyd's school c 480-510

Battle at Portsmouth 480

Brigit 480-525

Battle of Badon 495

Battle at Cammlan (Arthur killed) 515

Samson 525-563

Columba at Derry 544

Brendan's voyages 545 -560

Plague 547-551

David 550-589

Columba at Iona 563-597

Gildas in Ireland 565

Gregory the Great (Pope) 590-604

Augustine, Archbishop of Canterbury 597-604

Columbanus in Gaul, France and Italy 595-615

Edwin Baptised 625

Aidan at Lindisfarne 635-651

Hilda of Whitby 640-680

Synod at Whitby 664

Cuthbert died on Lindisfarne 687

CORNOVII KINGS

Conomorus (King Mark)

Lud	Tristan	Constantine	Crida

Lud
Geraint (Gerran)
Erbin (Ervan)

Constantine	Just	Selevan	Cyngar
		Cybi	

NORTHUMBRIAN KINGS

Edwin 617-633
Oswald 634-642 (killed by Penda)
Oswin killed by Oswy
Oswy 542-670 killed Penda 655

THE FRANKISH KINGS

CLOVIS.. KING OF FRANKS 481-511

CHILDEBERT I	CHILPERIC I	SIGIBERT I	LOTHAR I
496-558		King of Austrasia	King 511-561
		561-575	

m.Brunhilda

KINGDOM DIVIDED 561

LOTHAR II	CHILDERBERT II	GUNTRAM
584-629	born 570	532-92
king of Franks 613-29	king 575-596	king of Orleans 561

THEUDERBERT	THEODORIC
died 612	died 613